The Other Side of the Coin

A WORLD BANK STUDY

The Other Side of the Coin

The Comparative Evidence of Cash and In-Kind Transfers in Humanitarian Situations

Ugo Gentilini

WORLD BANK GROUP

Contents

Boxes

Figures

Tables

Acknowledgments

This book was produced as part of a broader initiative on humanitarian matters produced for the IASC by the World Bank (World Bank 2016a). The author is grateful for the support and strategic guidance of Colin Bruce, Jehan Arulpragasam, and Anush Bezhanyan, as well as Stephen Anderson and Matthew Hobson for technical advice and collaboration. Precious feedback was provided by Berk Ozler, David McKenzie, David Evans, Emanuela Galasso, Ruslan Yemtsov, Omar Arias, John Hoddinott, Harold Alderman, Jumana Qamruddin, Leslie Elder, Aline Coudouel, and Holger Kray.

About the Author

Ugo Gentilini is a senior economist with the Social Protection and Labor Global Practice at the World Bank. His interests encompass the analytics and practice of social protection, including as it relates, for example, to urbanization, humanitarian assistance, fragile states, food security and nutrition, and subsidy reforms. Before joining the World Bank in 2013, he spent more than a decade with the UN World Food Programme. He holds a PhD in development economics and has published on social protection matters in books, peer-reviewed journals, and the blogosphere.

Executive Summary

This paper reviews the existing evidence on the performance of alternative transfer modalities across humanitarian sectors, including cash transfers, vouchers, and in-kind assistance (food and non-food). These were assessed in relation to food security, nutrition, livelihoods, health, education, and shelter objectives. The analysis focuses on the *comparative* performance of transfers, that is, on robust studies assessing transfers against each other in the same context and objectives. Based on available evidence, the paper identifies key factors to consider for transfer selection and core research priorities. Overall, six main findings emerge.

Long-term global trends in concentration of people, economic activity, and technology are creating a landscape that is increasingly conductive for cash as an appropriate humanitarian response. The growing experiences with cash transfers over 2005–16 are promising, yet these seem dwarfed by their full potential. Trends in urbanization of crises and innovations in technology point to a possible significant increase in the share of cash used for humanitarian assistance beyond its current single-digit share.

In terms of evidence base, there is large variance in the availability of comparative evidence across sectors. This ranges from areas where evidence is substantial (that is, food security) to realms where it is limited (that is, nutrition) or where not a single comparative evaluation was available (that is, health, education, and shelter). This unbalance should be carefully considered when devising interventions and reforms that affect both single and multiple humanitarian sectors.

Where evidence is substantial, like for the food security cluster, data shows mixed results for cash and in-kind transfers, that is, their effectiveness is similar on average. Specific differences among cash and in-kind transfers are not very significant and depend on sub-objectives (for example, calories availability, dietary diversity) and indicators used to measure them. Also, transfers' performance and their difference seem a function of the organic and fluid interactions among a number of factors (for example, profile and "initial conditions" of beneficiaries, capacity of local markets), instead of inherent merits of a modality.

While the effectiveness of cash and in-kind is similar, the efficiency is generally in favor of cash. Cash transfers seem more efficient to *deliver* than in-kind modalities, suggesting it might be more cost-effective on average. However, results should be interpreted with caution, including because of the wealth of nuance that is often not captured in standard costs analysis. Delivery is only one dimension of cost assessments, and overall costs would hinge on the scale of interventions, crisis context, procurement practices, and hidden costs. Approaches for cost calculations are often not standardized and display high variance in the depth and breadth of analysis. More consistent and robust approaches are required so that efficiency analyses match the high-standards of effectiveness as offered by the examined impact evaluations. Whether in terms of effectiveness or efficiency, the use of combined transfers seems a promising and yet under-evaluated program model.

The appropriateness of transfers cannot be predetermined—there are no "first-best" options from the outset; rather, the best modalities are context-specific and emerge from response analysis. A range of factors should be considered for appropriate selection of transfer modalities. These have been extensively discussed the empirical and operational literature and include program objectives, the level of market functionality, predicted cost-effectiveness, implementation capacity, the management of key risks such as on protection and gender, political economy, beneficiary preferences, and resource availability. The depth and breadth of response analysis would range from basic analysis in the immediate aftermath of disasters, to more sophisticated and comprehensive processes as emergencies get prolonged and protracted.

Finally, it seems possible to reconcile humanitarian imperatives with solid research to inform decision-making. Given the nature of humanitarian situations, it is understandable that in many circumstances "action cannot wait for evidence." Notwithstanding humanitarian imperatives, as crises become more chronic and protracted there is an important case to be made to synchronize careful response analysis, operations, and a solid applied research agenda to compare performance of alternative transfer modalities. Many of the cases in challenging environments presented in the note, for example, Democratic Republic of Congo (DRC), Niger, and the Republic of Yemen, show that such analysis is possible and necessary to serve people in need in the best way possible.

Abbreviations

CCT	conditional cash transfer
DDI	Dietary Diversity Index
DRC	Democratic Republic of Congo
FAC	Food Aid Convention
FAO	Food and Agriculture Organization (of the UN)
FCS	Food Consumption Scores
GPRS	General Packet Radio Service
HDDS	Household Dietary Diversity Score
HIV	human immunodeficiency virus
IDPs	internally displaced persons
LESS	Logistics Execution Support System
MGA	multifaceted graduation approach
MPCT	multi-purpose cash transfers
NGO	nongovernmental organization
PDS	public food distribution system
PoS	point of sale
TCTR	total cost-transfer ratio
UNFPA	United Nations Population Fund
UNHCR	United Nations High Commissioner for Refugees
WFP	World Food Program
WHS	World Humanitarian Summit

CHAPTER 1

Introduction

Cash transfers are among the most rigorously evaluated fields in social sciences, including with a proven track record of performance in attaining intended objectives and second-round multipliers. Cash-based programs are now present in 130 developing countries, including representing between 30 and 70 percent of total safety net spending in those contexts (World Bank 2015). The basic question that this paper addresses, however, is not whether cash transfers work in general, but whether and when they do so *relative* to other transfer modalities. In particular, the paper examines such question with a humanitarian lens and across the sectors that form the humanitarian architecture.

Three modalities of transfers are here considered, namely cash, food, and vouchers. Cash transfers provide people with money, while in-kind transfers include the distribution of items as procured internationally or locally-sourced. Vouchers are also known as stamps or near-cash transfers and can be used in predetermined locations, including selected shops, supermarkets, retail stores, and fairs. Vouchers take two forms: on one hand, "value-based" vouchers restrict choice of items as available in the chosen outlet; on the other hand, vouchers can be "quantity-based," or tied to a pre-defined bundle of goods. Therefore, vouchers are a hybrid form of transfer that display features of both cash (value-based vouchers allow for some level of choice) and in-kind transfers (quantity-based vouchers are very similar to a decentralized system of local in-kind procurement). This basic taxonomy holds whether "in-kind" and vouchers refer to food, agricultural inputs, shelter, or other goods.

Somewhat unsurprisingly, the highest-quality evidence around the comparative performance of transfer modalities is generated in non-emergency contexts. The humanitarian situations in which multiple actors operate, characterized by the scale and urgency of required actions and the nature of impediments often present, is different from the conventional sphere of development interventions. Yet the field of humanitarian response is evolving rapidly, leading to greater focus on the generation of rigorous data on effectiveness, including solid impact evaluations. Indeed, humanitarian practitioners are increasingly called upon putting cash and in-kind transfers on an equal footing. This basically entails a more systematic consideration of alternative transfer modalities for a range of objectives and, as a result, across the sectors around which humanitarian assistance is "clustered." This is an important step since most of the eleven humanitarian clusters have limited experience with cash-based programs.

This imbalance in practice (and evidence) is important to recognize. When it comes to choice of transfer, sectors may share a range of common principles, but they may also face specific implications. While the literature on food assistance mostly antagonizes transfers as alternative modalities, there is some a priori resistance in, for example, considering cash in lieu of vaccines, therapeutic nutrition, or shelter. In other words, "how far should cash go" in being considered as an alternative or complement to in-kind assistance is a key strategic, operational and empirical question for the humanitarian community. Within such context, efforts are underway to ensure that the use of a certain transfer is not driven by reflexive approaches, that all transfer modalities should be considered more systematically, and that any choice is the result of careful response analysis. This paper, therefore, intends to contribute to the broader movement around making humanitarian choices contextual, objective-oriented, and evidence-based as much as possible.

The paper is organized as follows: the next chapter lays out a strategic overview of "where we come from," while the ensuing chapter 3 discusses the economics transfer modalities. In chapter 4, we assess the comparative impacts and costs of transfer modalities documented in solid impact evaluations. The discussion there revolves around food security, livelihoods, nutrition, health, education, shelter, and cross-sectoral approaches. Based on such analysis, chapter 5 lays out key issues to consider for transfer selection. Chapter 6 identifies evidence gaps and research priorities, while chapter 7 concludes.

CHAPTER 2

Positioning the Debate: A Strategic Perspective

This chapter briefly reviews strategic trends and historical roots of current transfer debates. In general, cash transfers still account for a minor share of humanitarian assistance, with nearly 94 percent of the humanitarian portfolio being provided in-kind (ODI 2015). This configuration is being increasingly challenged on many fronts, and the humanitarian architecture is recognizing the inherent limitations stemming from a low level of cash assistance. For example, the World Humanitarian Summit (WHS) Secretariat's Final Report on the WHS Global Consultations emphasized the need to "… generate a new architecture for supporting humanitarian cash transfers"; the recent High-Level Panel on Humanitarian Financing Report called for "… the use of unconditional and predictable cash in humanitarian settings to be rapidly scaled up," while the report of the Secretary-General for the WHS further recommended to "… use cash-based programming as the preferred and default method of support."

The fact that humanitarian assistance tends to gravitate around in-kind provisions has deep historical roots. For instance, over the 1960s and 1970s, a number of high-income countries nurtured generous systems of domestic agricultural subsidies. Such measures generated high surpluses of commodities which, in turn, were provided as in-kind food aid to developing countries facing deficits in food availability. In 1970, about 13.3 million tons of food aid were delivered globally, especially through trans-oceanic shipments. Institutional mechanisms such as the Food and Agriculture Organization of the UN (FAO) Consultative Subcommittee on Surplus Disposal, and later the Food Aid Convention (FAC), emerged and helped discipline the international use and commitments of in-kind assistance.

Throughout the 1980s and 1990s, reforms in donor approaches, especially in Europe, de-coupled the provision of international in-kind assistance from domestic agricultural goals. This reduced global in-kind food deliveries but, within such shrinking pool of in-kind resources, an increasing degree of flexibility was accorded to procure food in developing countries. As a result, the share of locally-procured in-kind commodities grew from 9 percent in 1990 to nearly 33 percent in 2005, including an increasing attention to the food quality and nutritional standards. Those procurement practices were the result of both greater flexibility in resources, but also of enhanced performance and larger transformations in agrifood systems. Growing per capita incomes and consumption patterns provided an entry point for organized, larger-scale retail outlets in urban markets, including as epitomized by the rapid rise of supermarkets across Africa and Asia.

Similar market conditions are likely to underpin humanitarian crises as they become more spatially concentrated. Urban areas host most the world's population and are expected to assimilate, by 2050, an additional 2.4 billion people, with 9 out of the 10 fastest-urbanizing countries being in Sub-Saharan Africa. While urban areas are often the engine of economic opportunity, they will also be increasingly exposed to disaster risks, which are projected to affect 870 million urban dwellers (Gentilini 2015).

The combination of functioning markets and flexible resources has led to an increase in the use of cash to respond to emergencies. For example, in 2005, cash was an important part of the response to the Indian Ocean tsunami, as well as being introduced in protracted crises (for example, Ethiopia) and conflict settings (for example, Somalia). By 2012, institutions such as the FAC gradually evolved into a broader platform, the Food Assistance Convention, which encompassed not only in-kind food (which dropped by over 60 percent from their 1970 level, including accounting for 4.7 million tons), but also cash transfers and vouchers (World Bank 2016a).

This growing diversity and flexibility in interventions was also reflected in the emergence of national social protection systems. Between 2010 and 2013, the number of African countries with unconditional cash transfers doubled, with those programs being currently present in 40 nations; similarly, the global spread of conditional cash transfers soared from 27 countries in 2008 to 64 in 2014 (World Bank 2015). Innovations in social protection are underway across low and middle-income countries, including in terms of building "systems" that are both robust and flexible. Indeed, social protection systems have been increasingly leveraged to help respond to humanitarian crises, including in contexts as diverse as Ethiopia, Philippines, Lebanon, Niger, and Palestine.

The evolution of technology has also provided favorable conditions for the use of cash. Increasingly, governments and donors are looking to transition their social protection payments from cash to electronic. This momentum toward e-payments rests on the promise of improving transparency, reducing leakage, and decreasing costs on the one hand, and facilitating value-added services for beneficiaries through financial access on the other. The rapid growth of mobile phones and point-of-sale devices has now created an opportunity to reach more poor people than ever before. For instance, nearly 7 of 10 people in the bottom fifth of the population in developing countries own a mobile phone, improving their access to markets and services. In Kenya, for example, the cost of sending remittances dropped by up to 90 percent after the introduction of M-Pesa, a digital payment system (World Bank 2016b).

Similarly, the price of biometric technology and smart cards has fallen to levels that make mass enrollment into electronic ID systems possible. Digital identity systems can provide better access to services for the 1.5 billion people who lack formal identification records, such as a birth certificate. This has been demonstrated recently in two of the world's largest countries, India and Indonesia. These are being used to open bank accounts, monitor attendance of civil servants, and identify recipients of government programs. Importantly, many of these technological innovations, for example, biometric verification of beneficiaries' identity, are sparking more efficient administration of programs *across* transfer modalities, including being applicable to cash, vouchers and in-kind transfers.

Despite the trends outlined above, in-kind assistance is likely to continue to be a strategically important component of humanitarian assistance in the years to come. Complex contextual situations during times of emergency will continue to call for in-kind support in specific instances. The interconnection of markets can present structural risks, including spreading crises swiftly and fueling volatility in prices of basic commodities. Connectivity and the penetration of technology is highly uneven across and within countries, often leaving the poorest and most vulnerable left behind. Both technological and social service delivery infrastructure and markets are often severely disrupted as a result of emergencies, or are seldom functional at adequate scale in complex crises and remote areas. And the critical nature of some objectives and activities pursued by the humanitarian community may not be achievable through local market mechanisms alone, for example, provision of vaccines and the treatment of severe malnutrition in some contexts. This is also an area where experimentation and evidence building should be prioritized.

Yet, taken together, the fundamental, long-term trends in concentration of people, economic activity, and technology is creating a landscape that is increasingly conductive for cash as an appropriate humanitarian response. The growing experiences with cash transfers over 2005–16 are promising, yet these seem dwarfed by their full potential. Trends in development and technology point to the scope to see a significant increase in the share of cash used for humanitarian assistance beyond its current share of 6 percent. This is reflected in the aspirations of the humanitarian community. Strategically aligning the composition of humanitarian assistance with evolving twenty-first century developments would allow for a more systematic consideration of cash on par with in-kind transfers.

Within this context, the use of cash transfers is, as mentioned, quite limited (6 percent of total humanitarian assistance); however, their use is on a clear upward pattern. For example, as of 2012 cash transfers reached 6.8 million beneficiaries (and 5.6 million in 2014), up from 2.4 in 2000. Over the same period, the quantity of global food aid halved, dropping from 10.9 to 4.7 million metric tons[1] (figure 2.1).

Figure 2.1 Trends in In-kind Food and Humanitarian Cash Transfers

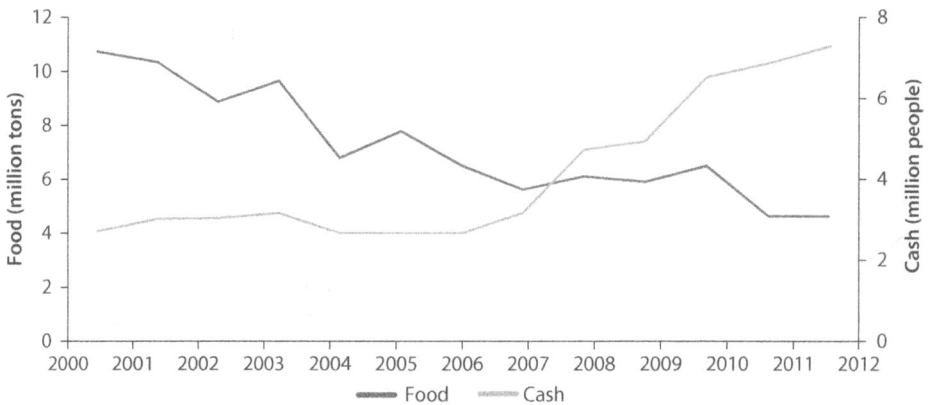

Source: CaLP-Cash Atlas and WFP-FAIS online databases (accessed January 2016).

Finally, it is important to also recognize that the provision of cash as humanitarian assistance can differ from that provided under national social safety nets. Notably, in 2014 only an estimated 3 percent, or US$ 1.1 billion, of total humanitarian funds was channeled through national governments (ALNAP 2015). As noted, this model of operating outside or with limited engagement of government systems can be dictated by several constraints. In general, however, such approach represents a departure from that of safety nets. The latter are typically provided through governments, including via blends of domestic resources, concessional financing, and medium/longer-term programmatic frameworks often embedded in national budgets. While the humanitarian and social protection worlds are increasingly connected (for example, through the use of common delivery platforms, risk financing mechanisms, etc.), whether cash or in-kind are provided as humanitarian assistance or a safety net can shape both design and policy implications (for example, whether those transfers are part of social contracts, etc.). Against this background, in the next chapter we start drilling into the cash versus in-kind debate, including starting from the economics of the quandary and then turning to their relative performance.

Note

1. The year 2012 is the last one for which data on food aid deliveries is recorded in the global Food Aid Information System housed by World Food Programme (WFP) (http://www.wfp.org/fais/).

CHAPTER 3

Choice and Paternalism: The Economics of Transfer Selection

Before assessing the evidence on comparative effectiveness, it is important to briefly discuss a set of cross-cutting issues affecting all transfer modalities. Among these, the issues of "paternalism" and choice permeate the debate in a way that makes is sometimes not only technically contentious, but even philosophically polarizing. This suggests the need for a short review of the economics of the cash versus in-kind debate, including with a view of shedding light on those thorny quandaries.

Standard economic theory predicts that cash is a preferable and first-best option, that is, cash is more "utility-maximazing" than in-kind transfers (Southworth 1945). This is a mainstream view in economics and has solid empirical grounds: for example, a survey showed that 84 percent of economists agree with the statement that "cash payments increase the welfare of recipients to a greater degree than do transfers-in-kind of equal cash value."[1] This stems from the basic feature that cash is flexible and provides people with choice on how to spend it. Relatedly, cash may not only transfer income, but transfer power as well. As it was put by Devarajan (2013), "… cash transfers have the potential to shift not just poverty-reducing policies but also the balance of power between government and its citizens, in favor of the latter." In other words, the normative argument in favor of cash is straightforward: cash is fungible and empowers, hence it is "transformative" or "redefinitional."[2] While these are important considerations, the economics of the quandary is more nuanced (Fraker et al. 1995).

Indeed, an economic case for in-kind transfers can also be made on the grounds of taxpayer utility functions, interdependent preferences, externalities, and information asymmetries—all of which somewhat rest on the notion of "paternalism" (Currie and Gahvari 2008). Part of the concept postulates that while members of society care about the worse-off and disadvantaged, the modeling of taxpayer functions can vary. For example, under one assumption taxpayers maximize their own utility when the poor are allowed to maximize their own happiness, that is, freely spend tax dollars. Under other assumptions, taxpaying voters typically exhibit a more parental form of altruism: they would like poor families to access a select few basic items (for example, food and housing) in adequate amounts, but specifically would not favor the poor to use tax-financed subsidies to purchase whatever goods and services.[3] This has been referred to as "specific egalitarianism" and postulates that while many people have no problem with income inequality per se, they would like to see that all individuals receive adequate food, medical services, or housing (Tobin 1970). In other words, the preference among voters for bestowing on the poor benefits-in-kind rather than cash transfers may well rest in good part on that characteristic of the typical tax payer's utility function (Reinhart 2013).

From another standpoint, the notion of paternalism revolves around "over-provision" of goods.[4] This involves informational, principal-agent, or behavioral arguments that often provide the foundations for much of the debate around conditionalities (Fiszbein and Schady 2009). In broad terms, the theory suggests that the expected externalities of an in-kind transfer would be desirable when there is a private under-investment—say, in nutrition or health—below an optimal social (or even private) level. Hence in-kind repre-senting a vehicle to influence behaviors, especially when people may not be well informed, may have inconsistent preferences over time, and there are coordination failures (De Mel, McKenzie, and Woodruff 2012). This is the case, for instance, when there is a discrepancy between perceived and expected returns, for example, to nutrition or education, which challenges the assump-tion that "people always know best."[5] For example, an experimental study by Jensen (2010) showed that students provided with information on returns to education completed 0.2 more years of schooling over the next 4 years compared to students without it.

From another perspective, there are questions around the core concept of "choice" by beneficiaries: is choice just the ability to freely dispose of a given transfer (for example, cash), or should such definition also include the oppor-tunity to choose what to get in the first place (for example, cash or food)? This is related to the thorny issue of what people prefer.[6] While it is difficult to generalize preferences, some stylized patterns can be discerned: for example, in-kind transfers tend to be preferred in the context of high or volatile prices, including due to seasonal or more unpredictable shocks (Sabates-Wheeler and Devereux 2010). Gender and intrahousehold decision making processes tend to be another key factor in shaping preferences, including the control that women exert over household in-kind or cash resources. Finally, people's preferences can be shaped by very pragmatic considerations, such as implementation perfor-mance of programs. In India, where the Public Food Distribution system (PDS) worked poorly people preferred cash, while they preferred food where existing food distributions were timely (Khera 2013). Somewhat relatedly, in some Indian states the use of technology in distribution has allowed beneficiaries to choose not necessarily what to get, but to select the service provider of preference[7] (Gentilini 2015).

In other words, "paternalism" is not necessarily a pejorative feature and can even be justified on economic grounds. Perhaps more generally, paternalism as an approach seems less related to modalities per se and more to processes to provide them. For instance, it can be argued that whether an intervention is paternalistic may hinge on the extent to which it considers beneficiaries as key stakeholders throughout the life of the program,[8] including balancing what might be desirable to provide from a public perspective and what beneficiaries would prefer to receive.

Notes

1. See Mankiw's blog posts at http://gregmankiw.blogspot.com/2009/02/news-flash-economists-agree.html, and http://gregmankiw.blogspot.com/2006/12/economics-of-gifts.html

2. Paul Niehaus, keynote address at the event "Cash Transfers: The New Benchmark for Foreign Aid?" hosted by the Center for Global Development (May 9, 2014, Washington, DC). Videos and materials of the event are available at: http://www.cgdev.org/event/cash-transfers-new-benchmark-foreign-aid.

3. See also the early work by, among others, Garfinkel (1973) and Amacher and Sandler (1977) exploring issues around paternalism and interdependent preferences.

4. In a stylized form, consider two individuals: for one, an in-kind transfer is defined as "extramarginal" because it is provided for an amount greater larger than the person would have normally consumed in the absence of the transfer; conversely, for another individual an in-kind transfer is inframarginal since it is smaller than the amount consumed by recipients. In other words, these two individuals are positioned in different points in the frontier of consumption possibilities. According to microeconomic models, an inframarginal in-kind transfer and a cash transfer of equal value would have the same effect in bolstering household food consumption—that is, beneficiaries' marginal propensity to consume food out of an additional income out of an in-kind or cash transfer should be the same. Put it differently, there is only an "income" effect and no "price" effect associated with inframarginal transfers. However, if in-kind transfers are extramarginal, then food consumption out of in-kind transfers would be larger than for an equal cash transfer due to the price effect. Yet economists have observed that in-kind transfers can be more effective than cash even when the former are inframarginal, which is referred to as 'cash-out puzzle'. For an elegant exposition of the theory, see Mankiw (2011). For a broader and thought-provoking reflection on the "economics of giving," see Mankiw (2006) and Reinhart (2013). For the empirical literature on the cash-out puzzle, see Basu (1996), Blackorby and Donaldson (1988), Breunig et al. (2001), Coate (1989), Faminow (1995), Fraker et al. (1995), Senauer and Young (1986).

5. For various examples in the health sector, see Currie and Gahvari (2008).

6. Note that the issue of expressing and capturing preferences is notoriously difficult, including due to a number of factors that may distort feedback such as how the question is posed, who conducts the survey, and expectations by beneficiaries.

7. The Chhattisgarh state in India has undergone a major reform of its Public Food Distribution (PDS) program. Between 2004 and 2010, the program was able to cut the share of people that "reported no PDS purchase" from 75 percent to 32 percent,

hence expanding coverage among eligible beneficiaries. Also, the diversion of PDS grains was reduced from 51 percent to 10.4 percent. Compounded with political commitment and other factors, a key ingredient behind Chhattisgarh's progress was the introduction of an automated system (COREPDS) in each participating fair price shop. This included the equipment of point of sale (PoS) devises with General Packet Radio Service (GPRS) connectivity, biometric authentication scanner, and smart card slot. The piloting of such system commenced in 2007, including 151 shops and 170,000 beneficiaries in Raipur city. Differently from the previous models, it allowed beneficiaries to choose the shop where to access the benefits. In other words, benefits were made portable. This introduced a strong element of competition among shopkeepers and, as early evidence shows, a number of challenges with underprovision were eliminated. While comprehensive evaluations are underway, the experience suggests that technology alone can improve but not fully address issues of transparency. The pilot instead shows that the empowerment of participants through choice (as provided by portability) was a key determinant in elevating people "from beneficiaries to customers," hence letting market mechanisms and competition to largely address previous inefficiencies.

8. For example, in 2006 a combined cash and food transfer program was implemented in rural Malawi. The follow-up evaluation explored participants' preferences over one or both transfers and found that "… most beneficiaries were very satisfied with receiving both food and cash" (Devereux 2008). Yet, the redesign of the project in 2007 only envisaged cash transfers.

CHAPTER 4

Comparative Performance across Sectors

Food Security

Programs intended for food security have played a dominant role in shaping views on cash versus in-kind modalities, albeit through a narrower "cash versus food" lens. For instance, **over 2010–15 a total of 788 projects** were implemented by the humanitarian community, including reaching **29 million beneficiaries** for a value of over USD 3.9 billion. Out of this portfolio, over half or 56 percent were implemented around the food security sector.[1]

We examine the complete set of robust impact evaluations that, to our knowledge,[2] have been published over the last decade, 2006–16 (Gentilini 2016). These include 14 comparative experimental and quasi-experimental trials in 11 developing countries that have deliberately compared alternative transfer modalities under the same evaluation framework. The specific design parameters of the programs are presented in appendix A. Some of the case studies include stable contexts, such as Bangladesh, Cambodia, Malawi, and Mexico, but most of them are particularly relevant to inform humanitarian debates. These include evaluations fielded in Uganda's fragile Karamoja region, Ecuador's periurban program for Colombian refugees, the project in the Democratic Republic of Congo (DRC) for internally displaced populations, crisis-affected regions in the Republic of Yemen, Ethiopia's high food prices-induced emergency, drought-hit regions in Niger, and post-tsunami Sri Lanka (Ahmed et al. 2010; Aker 2015; Barker, Filmer, and Rigolini 2014; Cunha 2014; Gilligan and Roy 2013; Hidrobo et al. 2014b; Hoddinott, Sandstrom, and Upton 2014; Leroy et al. 2010; Schwab 2013; Sharma 2006; Skoufias, Unar, and Gonzalez-Cossio 2008).

A summary of the impacts is proposed in table 4.1, including displaying the most effective transfer modality according to different dimensions. The absolute differences in impacts are reported in appendix B. Overall, cash was most effective in achieving specific objectives 48 percent of the time, and food was so in 36 percent of the cases. Vouchers and combined cash and food modalities were

Table 4.1 Summary of Impacts from Comparative Food Security Studies

	Transfers Provided	More Effective Modality							
		Food Consumption	Calorie Intake	Food Gap	Dietary Diversity	Poverty	Anemia	Child Malnutrition	Child Mortality
Bangladesh	Cash, food	Cash	Cash	–	–	Food	–	–	–
Cambodia	Cash, food	Cash	–	–	Food	–	–	–	–
Congo, Rep.	Cash, vouchers	Vouchers	–	–	Cash	–	–	–	–
Ecuador	Cash, food, vouchers	Food	Food	–	Vouchers	–	–	–	–
Ethiopia	Cash, food			Food			–	–	–	–
Malawi	Cash, food, cash + food	–	–	–	Cash	–	–	–	–
Mexico	Cash, food	Cash	Food	–	–	Food	–	–	–
Niger*	Cash, food	–	–	–	Food	–	–	–	–
Niger**	Cash, food, cash + food	–	–	–	–	–	–	Cash + food	Cash + food
Sri Lanka	Cash, food	Cash	Cash	–	–	–	–	–	–
Uganda	Cash, food	–	–	Cash	–	–	Cash	–	–
Yemen, Rep.	Cash, food	Cash	Food	–	Cash	–	–	–	–

Source: Ahmed et al. (2010), Aker (2015), Barker et al. (2014), Cunha (2014), Gilligan and Roy (2013), Hidrobo et al. (2014a), Leroy et al. (2010), Schwab (2013), Sharma (2006), Skoufias et al. (2008), Hoddinott, Sandstrom, and Upton (2014), Langendorf et al. (2014)
Note: "–" means that impacts of modalities are either similar or not reported; dietary diversity is measured by the dietary diversity index, except for Cambodia and DRC where it was measured by food consumption scores and household dietary diversity scores, respectively; DRC = Democratic Republic of Congo; Niger* = Hoddinott, Sandstrom, and Upton (2014), Niger**= Langendorf et al. (2014), see nutrition section.

the most effective in the remaining 16 percent of the times, which is remarkable given that those modalities were used only in few cases. The potential and likely underexplored effectiveness of mix of modalities mirrors the findings by Maunder et al. (2015), including reporting that combined transfers exceeded a donor's (ECHO) target results in one-quarter of the cases.[3]

One of the most widely used indicators in the examined compilation of evaluations is food consumption. Collected in 7 out of the 11 countries, food consumption was measured in terms of expenditures or value of food consumed at household level.[4] Only in Ecuador impacts of food consumption were larger for food-receiving beneficiaries, including relative to both cash and voucher transfers. In the Republic of Yemen, Cambodia, Mexico, Sri Lanka and Bangladesh the impacts on food consumption are higher for cash than for food-beneficiary households. In the case of Bangladesh, one possible explanation is that the size of the cash transfer was 70 percent higher than the food transfer. In the Republic of Yemen, Cambodia, and Sri Lanka, the difference in percentage points was double digit. However, the difference in impacts is statistically significant only for the Republic of Yemen and Sri Lanka. In DRC, cash households spent approximately US$ 0.34 less than voucher households on food, or about US$ 0.11 less per capita. This was largely due to the fact that vouchers were commodity-based.

Measures for quantifying calorie in-take may present additional information regarding the difference in impacts on food availability at household level. In contrast with measures of food consumption, food transfers tend to have a larger impact on calorie in-take relative to cash in most contexts. In Ecuador, the larger effect on calories from food was mainly due to larger increases in consumption of cereals (which represented 41 percent of households' caloric intake). In Republic of Yemen, higher caloric consumption from food stemmed from the basket composition, including wheat and oil. In the case of Sri Lanka, cash had a larger impact than food. Such effect can be explained by a change in diets, that is, a shift in consumption from highly caloric foods to diets of higher-quality (for example, eggs, meat). In the case of Mexico, the result is consistent with another study by Leroy et al. (2010) showing that, compared to the cash group, the effect of food was higher for total energy, energy from animal-source foods, and energy from cereals and legumes. According to the authors, this was most likely due to the fact that the food basket contained relatively large quantities of grains and legumes.[5]

Another reviewed indicator is the food gap, which measures months of food shortage by households. In the case of Ethiopia, a two year exposure to food rations led to less months of food shortage compared to household participating in cash transfers. In Uganda, among cash and food treated household there was a reduction of 0.6 and 0.4 months of food insecurity respectively. However, the difference is not statistically significant.

In order to explore the quality of consumption patterns and diets, evaluations have analyzed dietary diversity indicators. Three include the Dietary Diversity Index (DDI), Food Consumption Scores (FCS) and Household Dietary Diversity Score (HDDS).[6] Results on FCS in Cambodia, Niger (July and October), Ecuador and Republic of Yemen. Results are mixed, with cash being more effective in three cases (Ecuador's cash and vouchers arms and Republic of Yemen), and food in the other three (Cambodia and Niger, both seasons). In Ecuador, the larger increase in dietary diversity for vouchers was mainly due to larger increases in the number of days consuming vegetables, eggs, milk and dairy. Similar effects of transfers were noted for the DDI, which included the same sample of countries except Cambodia. One reason that the cash recipients had less diverse diets lies in their choice of using a significant proportion of their transfers to buy grains in bulk, the least expensive form of calories present on local markets. As it was pointed out by Hoddinott, Sandstrom, and Upton (2014), such purchasing strategy was a reflection of uncertainty regarding future food prices (as well as being easier at harvest).

The two studies in DRC and Ecuador also allowed for comparing dietary diversity among cash and voucher-receiving arms. In the former, cash households used their transfer to purchase a more diverse set of food and non-food items. In particular, cash program recipients were significantly more likely to purchase staple grains (a 24 percentage point increase), beans (a 38 percentage point increase), condiments (a 27 percentage point increase), as well as oil, meat and vegetables as compared to the voucher group. Vouchers, instead, directed or restricted household purchasing decisions toward specific food items, including voucher recipients being 10 percentage points more likely to purchase other grains (namely rice) and 13 percentage points more likely to purchase salt than cash recipients.

In Ecuador, the impact among cash and voucher recipients was considerably lower. Bearing in mind the difference in the size and frequency of the voucher transfers,[7] cash-receiving households not only invested large share of the transfer for food (83 percent), but the money was used to purchase various foods across 7 groups (rots and tubers, vegetables, meat and poultry, eggs, fish and seafood, pulses and legumes, and milk and diary). Yet vouchers led to increases in 9 out of 12 food groups and, compared to cash, it sparked an increase in the frequency of consumption of fish and seafood, and pulses and legumes. Instead, in the DRC vouchers were used for a variety of food purchases, while cash transfers were more likely to be used for alternative purposes, such as for paying for school fees or being saved.[8]

Finally, a key dimension of food security is "access" to food, hence being closely related to income and monetary poverty issues. The evidence showed that both food and cash transfers reduced poverty in Mexico and Bangladesh. In Mexico and Bangladesh, estimates on the impacts of cash and food transfers on the extreme poverty headcount ratio show that food had larger impacts, with a difference on 3.8 and 1.9 percentage points in Bangladesh and Mexico, respectively (Ahmed et al. 2010; Skoufias, Unar, and Gonzalez-Cossio 2008). The overall impacts of transfers on the poverty gap are larger. In the context of Mexico, food transfers decreased the poverty gap by 22.3 percent and cash transfers by 18.9 percent; moreover, the severity of poverty decreased by 27.8 and 22.9 percent, respectively.

A number of factors affect the comparative efficiency of cash, vouchers and in-kind transfers. These include the scale of the intervention, the type of humanitarian crisis, delivery mechanisms, transfer size, procurement costs, and a range of "hidden" costs. We'll briefly discuss these factors individually. For example, in a comprehensive evaluation of ECHO's cash and vouchers portfolio, Maunder et al. (2015) assessed the cost-efficiency of 163 transfer projects through the use of an index called Total Cost-Transfer Ratio (TCTR). Such indicator measures the cost of delivering one dollar worth of transfer to a beneficiary, that is, the more the TCTR exceeds unity, the less cost-efficient the program is.[9] The analysis by Maunder et al. (2015) estimated that larger-scale projects were in general more efficient than smaller projects. Because in-kind projects were between 6 and 16 times larger than other modalities, the *average* TCTR for sampled in-kind programs was lower than for other modalities. However, the data suggest that, once at scale, cash transfers are more efficient than in-kind transfers (table 4.2).

Table 4.2 Cost of Transfer Modalities by Scale of Operations

Beneficiaries ('000)	Cash	Vouchers	In-kind	Combinations	Total
<10	2.72	3.23	2.40	1.82	2.74
10–50	1.46	1.87	1.86	2.08	1.70
50–100	1.30	1.44	1.55	2.37	1.70
100–500	1.28	1.36	2.05	1.68	1.60
>500	n.a.	n.a.	1.63	–	1.63
Average	1.93	2.11	1.84	2.03	1.96
Number of cases	76	34	30	23	163

Source: Maunder et al. (2015).
Note: n.a. = not applicable

Table 4.3 Cost of Transfer Modalities by Humanitarian Context

Context	Cash	Vouchers	In-kind	Combinations	Total
Complex emergency	2.81	2.11	1.86	2.33	2.37
Slow onset	1.64	1.54	2.44	1.96	1.81
Sudden onset	1.39	2.72	1.46	1.61	1.62
Refugees	1.15	1.81	1.48	1.40	1.44
Average	1.93	2.11	1.84	2.03	1.96
Number of cases	76	34	30	23	163

Source: Maunder et al. (2015).

Also, the evaluation showed that the operating context can significantly influence the average TCTR of the different modalities. Overall, TCTR values were highest in complex emergencies, followed by slow onset natural disasters (for example, drought), then rapid onset natural disasters (for example, other extreme weather events, earthquakes) and lowest in refugee responses. It is hypothesized that the high costs of complex emergencies are related to increased operating costs (such as security), whilst well established refugee settings allow the greatest opportunity for cost savings through forward planning and longer term distributions. A possible explanation for rapid onset disaster response having a lower TCTR than slow onset is that the former tend to occur in countries with less developed infrastructure and markets. Whilst cash transfers usually have the lowest TCTR in most contexts, data shows it has the highest TCTR in complex emergencies. The TCTR for vouchers is also significantly higher in responding to sudden onset disasters (table 4.3).

When assessing efficiency, it is also useful to distinguish between the delivery of assistance and other cost items. Delivery is here defined as encompassing costs related to "moving" transfers from the agency to beneficiaries. These may include transportation, handling and storage of food, as well as costs related to benefit payment, for example, debit card fees per transaction, printing of vouchers or issuance of magnetic cards. In this regard, our findings corroborate those of Cabot Venton, Bailey, and Pongracz (2015) in that cash, when compared to in-kind approaches, consistently emerges as more efficient to *deliver* (see table 4.4). Put it differently, Margolies and Hoddinott (2015) estimated that at the particular levels of transfers in four studies that compared equal value of transfers, between 13 and 23 percent additional households could have been reached if the food transfers were in cash instead.

In terms of cost of "transfers" as opposed to just delivery, it is important to contrast the cost for agencies and the local value of such transfer for beneficiaries. For cash transfers, the issue is straightforward: the cost of the transfer and its local value are always the same, that is, the procurement cost of cash is exactly the amount of cash provided to beneficiaries. Indeed, in most food assistance projects the size of cash transfers is generally calculated as the monetary value of a bundle of food commodities on local markets.

When it comes to food transfers, costs for agencies and local market values may not be the same. Specifically, there might be economies of scale from purchasing large quantities of commodities from producers, wholesale traders, and, in the case of vouchers, small retailers.[10] In other words, under the right circumstances agencies can "buy low and transfer high": if the difference between the purchase cost and the recipient transfer value is large enough, such differences can offset possible delivery cost savings from cash transfers, such as observed in Malawi, Niger, and Palestine (Audsley et al. 2010; Creti 2011). An illustration with data from two projects is proposed in box 4.1.

Devising robust and standardized tools and methods for identifying, collecting and analyzing cost data should be a key priority for the transfer debate. In this regard, it'd be important that cost calculations are based on a more nuanced understanding of supply chains and agricultural markets. Indeed, implementation models can vary considerably pending on the specific

Table 4.4 Summary of Efficiency from Comparative Food Security Studies

	Transfers Provided	More Efficient Modality		
		Delivery Cost	Transfer Cost	Overall Efficiency
Bangladesh	Cash, food	Cash	n.a.	Cash
Congo, Rep.	Cash, vouchers	Cash	n.a.	Cash
Ecuador	Cash, food, vouchers	Cash	Cash	Cash
Yemen Rep.	Cash, food	Cash	Food	Food
Uganda	Cash, food	Cash	n.a.	Cash
Niger*	Cash, food	Cash	n.a.	Cash
Niger**	Cash, food, cash + food	Cash	Food	Food
Malawi	Cash, food, cash + food	n.a.	Food	Food
Mexico	Cash, food	Cash	n.a.	Cash

Source: Ahmed et al. (2010), Aker (2015), Cunha (2014), Gilligan and Roy (2013), Hidrobo et al. (2014a), Leroy et al. (2010), Schwab (2013), Hoddinott, Sandstrom, and Upton (2014), Langendorf et al. (2014)
Note: Niger* = Hoddinott, Sandstrom, and Upton (2014), Niger**= Langendorf et al. (2014), n.a. = not applicable.

Box 4.1 Procurement Versus Delivery Costs: Evidence from Ecuador and the Republic of Yemen

Let's illustrate these considerations by contrasting results between two countries. In Ecuador, the procurement costs for food were higher than their local market value: indeed, accounting for the local procurement of most of canned fish, rice, lentils and oil, and including the international procurement of some oil and lentils, it turns out that it cost USD 46.76 to provide a transfer that is locally-valued at USD 40. This led to a total cost of providing food of USD 58.25 (USD 46.76 + 11.46), which even exacerbated the cost differences—that is, total cost for cash is USD 42.99 while for vouchers is USD 43.27 (the value of both voucher and cash transfer is, by definition, USD 40). Indeed, the difference between food and cash is now USD 15.26 per transfer compared to USD 8.47 (that is, USD 11.46 – USD 2.99) when transfer values were excluded. In the Republic of Yemen, instead, the market conditions were such that it was possible to procure for USD 39 a food basket locally valued at USD 49. In this case, the cost difference between food and cash cost even reversed, with cash being USD 2.8 more expensive than food (figure 4.1).

Figure 4.1 Difference in Total Costs Between Transfer Modalities, with and Without Procurement Analysis

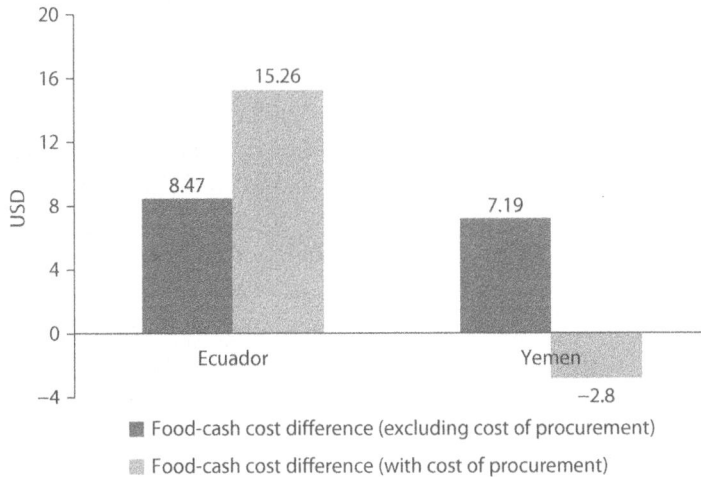

Source: Margolies and Hoddinott (2014).

approaches and actors involved at different points in supply chains. For instance, Gelli and Suwa (2014) noted that:

> different approaches can even co-exist within the same country, where, for instance, programme implementation is owned by decentralised institutions (e.g. individual states in Brazil or India), or where agencies (…) are complementing the national programmes (e.g. Ghana and Kenya), [or models] linking the provision of goods and services for school feeding to smallholder farmers and the community.

Those nuances need to be taken into account for comprehensive cost analyses, and so would a range of hidden costs.

Indeed, one key issue for program efficiency relates to the time, forgone income and transportation costs that people may incur to access the benefit. For example, Margolies and Hoddinott (2014) estimated that in the Republic of Yemen, cash was more efficient than food for the agency, but not for beneficiaries: it cost 2.7 hours of travel/waiting time and high transportation costs (8.6 percent of transfer value) to access cash, as opposed to 1.9 hours and 2 percent of transfer's value for transportation cost for accessing food. This is because food was distributed closer to people's villages, which increased the cost for the agency and lowered that of beneficiaries. In Ecuador, instead, food distribution sites were located farther than cash and voucher payment points, hence increasing private costs (in terms of both time and income); in Uganda and Niger, there appears to be no difference in transaction costs since both transfers were distributed at village-level.

In general, there appears to be a trade-off between costs for the implementer and those for beneficiaries: as payment or distribution points get closer to beneficiaries, costs for the implementer get higher, while the transaction costs for beneficiaries dwindle. In other words, programs that seem less expensive could be so because the cost of accessing transfers had been shifted from the implementer to the beneficiary.

Efficiency is also influenced by whether cash is provided as a substitute for in-kind assistance or whether in addition to it (that is, when agencies can operate both cash and in-kind delivery system). For example, a refugee program in Ethiopia replaced a portion of the in-kind basket with cash. Data suggest that cash was 25–30 percent cheaper to deliver than in-kind aid (Cabot Venton, Bailey, and Pongracz 2015). Many of the gains of cash transfers arise because the agency delivering food did not set up a separate system for cash, but rather maintained efficiency by using the existing food delivery system. Similarly, in Lebanon World Food Programme's (WFP's) corporate relationship with Mastercard and the bank with which it partnered resulted in waived fees for certain costs, and economies of scale and competition led a card service company working with United Nations High Commissioner for Refugees (UNHCR) partners to reduce costs associated with ATM-distributed cash.

In a range of circumstances, beneficiaries receiving food transfers may resale them in full or in part in local markets. This may happen not necessarily because food was not needed per se, but because the need to meet non-food expenditure priorities (for example, medicines) or for buying foods of different quality. While a comprehensive review of resales of commodities may not be available, anecdotal evidence suggest that the practice mat occur in a number of contexts. Given that resales may entail transaction costs by beneficiaries and sales may occur at prices below market ones (and at a cost below that of procurement incurred by the agency), it would be important to document and quantify those practices more systematically and include them in cost analyses.

Finally, the potentially large logistics costs entailed by food-based programs, including procurement, transport, storage, and distribution, may posit particular risks for accountability, transparency and "leakages." In India, for example, it was estimated that, in the early 2000s, about 58 percent of the food under the Targeted Public Distribution System did not reach the intended beneficiaries (World Bank 2011). Such losses throughout the logistics chain should also be accounted for comprehensive cost-effectiveness assessments of alternative modalities.

Livelihoods and Entrepreneurship

In order to gauge the appropriateness of providing cash grants to enhance earning opportunities, it's important to identify key constraints faced by the poor. These might include market failures around labor markets (for example, information to match skills and job opportunities), credit and capital constraints, lack of coordination among different actors involved in job markets, and low individual capacities (for example, lack of information, cognitive and psychological limitations). These represent forms of barriers that may demand distinct government interventions (Almeida, Behrman, and Robalino 2012).

Specifically, the choice between cash and in-kind transfers for livelihoods tends to occur when people's main constraint is lack of capital or an individual limitation. In other words, "in-kind" here refers to physical capital, assets, materials, or training.[11] A range of interventions providing mostly-cash or mostly in-kind grants have been implemented and evaluated, often as part of "graduation" approaches (see box 4.2). These are not necessarily "pure" cash or in-kind grants, but provide a blend of cash and in-kind interventions in different proportions.

Box 4.2 Cash and In-kind-Based Grants

Among cash-oriented grants, the Northern Uganda Social Action Funds Uganda targeted mostly young males (mean age of 25), underemployed, and with above median wealth and education (75 percent had primary school education) in a credit constrained environment (Blattman, Fiala, and Martinez 2014). Participants formed groups of 20 individuals and submitted investment proposals, with selected ones receiving an average transfer of USD 382 per group. This was not an unconditional cash transfer per se, since proposals should include training and capital investment components. After 4 years, large improvements were shown in skilled trade, work hours and earnings. However, a similar program in Tanzania targeted to "vulnerable households" did not have same success (Ozler 2015). Also, less pronounced findings for cash grants to young people were found in Liberia (Blattman, Jamison, and Sheridan 2015).

Among in-kind-oriented grants, a prominent one is the Multifaceted Graduation Approach (MGA). This provides "ultra-poor" beneficiaries with productive assets (for example, livestock), training and support for those asset, life skills coaching, consumption

---

box continues next page

Box 4.2 Cash and In-kind-Based Grants *(continued)*

support with cash or food for about a year, access to savings accounts, and health information and services. In other words, as opposed to cash-oriented grants, MGA offers intense
"hand-holding" toward graduation and mostly through in-kind transfers. After a year from
the program's end, Banerjee et al. (2015) assessed six country case studies and found significant effects across the board (consumption, income, food security, asset accumulation,
mental health, political involvement, etc.). Yet the size of the effect sizes were modest[12]
(0.05–0.25 SD). The total program costs for the full duration of the program ranged from
US$1,455 per household (India) to US $5,962 (Pakistan). Transfers accounted for about a
third of total direct costs, but with high variation (19 percent in Ghana to 63 percent in India). After two years from program completion, a study by Bandiera et al. (2012) for Bangladesh found similar effects on asset accumulation, expenditures, earnings, and life satisfac-
tion. They also found a significant shift from wage labor to self-employment, with growing
hours worked and hourly wages increasing. A simulated comparison to a hypothetical
equal-valued cash grant was favorable to an in-kind MGA.

As in the food security realm, evidence from a direct comparison of cash versus
in-kind transfers within the same intervention is more limited and available only
for a handful of countries (see table 4.5 for a summary). These found that cash
grants alone were not always the most effective modality, while in-kind or combinations of modalities could at times do better. A limitation of these studies is
that many of them have insufficient statistical power to rule out large differences
between cash and in-kind. Comparative cost analysis is also rarely available.

In particular, in Uganda Fiala (2013) evaluated a program for business owners
who were randomly selected to receive loans, cash grants, business skills training
or a combination of these programs. Six and nine months after the interventions,
men with access to loans with training report 54 percent greater profits. The
loan-only intervention had some initial impact, but this dissipated by the nine
months follow-up. No significant impacts were found from the unconditional
grant interventions but the confidence intervals allow for relatively large effects.

In urban Ghana, Fafchamps et al. (2014) randomly gave cash and in-kind
grants to male and female-owned microenterprises. For women running subsistence enterprises, there were no gains in profits from either treatment. For
women with larger businesses, only in-kind grants caused growth in profits, suggesting a flypaper effect whereby "… capital coming directly into the business
sticks there, but cash does not." However, for men the authors cannot reject that
cash and in-kind grants have the same effect.

Finally, two different experiments were conducted in Sri Lanka. In the first
one, De Mel, McKenzie, and Woodruff (2008) evaluated the effects on firms of
the provision of capital stock on business profits. The median firm owner in the
sample was 41 years old, had 10 years of education, and had been running his or
her firm for 5 years. Participants were provided with capital in cash or in-kind

Table 4.5 Summary of Evidence from Comparative Livelihood Studies

	Transfers Provided	Most Effective Modality	Comments
Uganda	Cash, loans, in-kind (trainings), combinations	Loans + in-kind	Program designed for business owners
Ghana	Cash, in-kind (equipment, materials)	In-kind	Effects only for larger business-owners
Sri Lanka	Cash, in-kind (training), Cash + in-kind	Cash + in-kind	Effects only for women already in business
Bangladesh	Cash, in-kind (full graduation package)	In-kind	Estimates for cash based on simulations

Source: Bandiera et al. (2012), Del Mel et al. (2012), Fafchamps et al. (2014), Fiala (2013)

(equipment). The study found that those forms of capital had similar effects and increased profits of microenterprises by over 5 percent per month, or at least 60 percent per year. However, these effects only occurred for men, with no impact of either in-kind or cash grants for women.

In the second experiment, De Mel, McKenzie and Woodruff (2012) assed the performance of business training with and without cash grants among two groups of women: one operating subsistence enterprises and the other who were out of the labor force but interested in starting a business. After 2 years, for women already in business, training alone had no impact on business profits, sales or capital stock. In contrast, a mix of training and grant led to large and significant improvements in business profitability, although impacts dissipated over time. For women interested in starting enterprises, business training accelerated labor market entry but showed no increase in net business ownership. Both profitability and business practices of the new entrants are increased by training, suggesting training may be more effective for new owners than for existing businesses.

In general, this brief discussion points to the importance to understand which constraint binds: cash or in-kind grant programs can likely be effective when the key constraint is lack of capital or of information/skills, but not others. Also, objectives and targeting matter: some of the most successful grant programs (for example, Uganda) targeted relatively educated and wealthy youth. Programs targeting the poorest and vulnerable generated more limited impacts. Finally, only a handful of programs have deliberately compared cash and in-kind interventions, and relative cost-efficiency data is limited.

Nutrition

The determinants of child malnutrition are multifaceted and involve a range of issues around access to food, feeding practices, and broader environmental and sanitary conditions. This is important to underscore since transfers should be mostly interpreted in relation to the component around access to (nutritious) food as a key cause of malnutrition. In this regard there is a significant research gap in exploring the ability of alternative transfers to achieve nutritional goals.[13]

Indeed, as laid out by Webb et al. (2014) the specific interventions to pursue those goals largely or almost entirely include in-kind approaches. These include general food assistance, management of severe and moderate acute malnutrition, delivery of micronutrient, infant and young child feeding in emergencies, treatment of diarrhea with oral rehydration therapy/zinc, prevention and treatment of vitamin a deficiency, food and nutrition assistance for people living with human immunodeficiency virus (HIV), the psychosocial components of nutrition, and nutritional care for groups with special needs. Similarly, a recent Cochrane review by Pega et al. (2015) concluded that "… compared with in-kind food, there was no evidence that cash influenced the chance of child death or severe acute malnutrition."

However, some studies present data on relative impacts of transfers on short and longer-term nutrition-related dimensions. In Mexico, both food and cash transfers increased the in-take of micronutrient (iron) amongst children by 1.61 and 1.10 milligram, respectively. However, the difference is not statistically significant. The same pattern holds for increases in zinc and vitamin C. Anemia prevalence was reduced by 2 percent in food-receiving households and 4 percent in the cash arm. In Uganda, cash decreased anemia by about 10 percentage points among children (at 10 percent confidence level). In this context, food transfers had no significant impact. In Cambodia neither treatment modality in the food-cash scholarship program had significant impacts on anthropometric indicators, possibly because of the small transfer size and short exposure to treatment.

The most robust and recent study in humanitarian settings includes a perspective study in Niger's region of Maradi (Langendorf et al. 2014). The study compared several types of cash and food combinations—including a rage of different high-quality foods (for example, lipid-based supplements and fortified cereals) as well as more traditional ones (oil, pulses)—with the objectives to reduce severe and moderate acute malnutrition as well as mortality rates among children. The findings indicated that combining food and cash transfers reduced the incidence of malnutrition at about twice the rate compared to either a cash transfer or to supplementary food alone.

Health

Just like nutrition, the determinants of health are complex and multidimensional. Health can be considered a broader domain than nutrition, with issues such as morbidity and child malnutrition being key causes of child health and mortality. Those domains underscore the importance of the quality and availability of services: while the cash versus in-kind transfer debate is largely about "demand-side" issues, there is a much wider agenda around the supply-side of services, with health being at the center of it (UNHCR 2015). In other words, the issue is closely related to the debate around conditionality in transfers, including when they are appropriate, the type of conditions, and degree of enforcement.[14]

While an extensive discussion on conditionality goes beyond the scope of this note, the issue stresses the importance of understanding causality chains and the role of transfers within them. In other words, transfers cannot replace services, and when it comes to health, their quality and availability are key in influencing the effectiveness and efficiency of transfer-based interventions—whether in cash or in-kind. For instance, while transfer programs have been successful in increasing utilization of health services, the subsequent link that programs improve the health of the population is not always evident in the data (Meyer et al. 2011).

Although in the nutrition field we were able to document at least a few comparative studies of alternative modalities, in the health sector there seems to be a dearth of relative evidence. Although some experience exists (see box 4.3), a comprehensive evaluation concluded "… there is no documentation on the cost efficiency or cost effectiveness of using cash transfers,

---

Box 4.3 Vouchers for Emergency Health and Sanitation

Vouchers for reproductive health in the Syria Arab Republic were implemented by United Nations Population Fund (UNFPA) and funded by ECHO. The vouchers enabled women to obtain free-of-charge maternal and obstetric services at the Obstetric University Hospital and Syrian Family Planning Association clinics. The vouchers widened the spectrum of health centres, which increased the chances of beneficiaries to get services. In 2012 and 2013, UNFPA distributed around 40,000 vouchers in violence-affected areas through outreach mobile teams or medical volunteers providing reproductive health services and information. The distribution was systematic and focused not only on shelters for Internally Displaced Persons (IDPs) but also in most needed communities through nongovernmental organizations (NGOs) mobile teams and medical professionals working in the most affected communities in the targeted governorates in Damascus, Rural Damascus, Homs and Aleppo. The services covered by RH vouchers include mainly emergency and life-saving activities (C-section, hysterectomy, bleeding). In Gaza, a voucher was introduced in 2012 over a three-month period to cover the drinking water needs of 696 households. In particular, the voucher provided access to 6.5 liters of chlorinated and desalinated water per person/day provided by water vendors (truckers). In Lebanon, Syrian refugees families sharing household latrines (270 latrines, each shared by three families) were given a $30 commodity voucher that enabled them to empty their latrines via a local contractor (market actor) identified by NGOs and their partners. In the aftermath of the 2010 Haiti earthquake and following a market assessment, a commodity voucher programme was introduced to provide 440 households with essential hygiene items through local shops. The vouchers could be exchanged through seven contracted shops for a fixed quantity of specified hygiene commodities. In Jordan, about 3,000 households were provided with a voucher value of USD 21. This could be redeemed in 11 contracted shops against a relatively broad selection of hygiene items, including soap, buckets, baby diapers, and others.

Source: Maunder et al. (2015).

---

vouchers or value-based vouchers in providing health services during humanitarian crisis" (Gorter et al. 2012). This might be due to the unfamiliarity among health workers with these tools, the complex determinants of health, and the need to ensure quality in provision.

Education

Many of the considerations advanced for health and nutrition can apply to education as well. Being a service, also education rests on both supply and demand-side issues: where the former include things like classrooms, text books, and quality of education, the latter includes transfers that incentivize the usage of a specific service (that is, schools). Also in this case, we find that sequence and preconditions matter—there is little rationale (beyond political economy) to implement a conditional transfer if the supply of services is unavailable or of inadequate quality.

On a related point, in Tanzania there is extensive experimental evidence documenting the effectiveness of national Conditional cash transfers (CCT) programs (Evans et al. 2014). However, polls show that 92 percent of a sampled Tanzanian voters would rather spend government revenues on supply-side services (including education) rather than cash transfers (Sandefur, Birdsall, and Moyo 2015). One reason respondents cited for favoring government services over direct distribution was that social services encourage a collective voice that helps increase accountability, while transfers would focus people on private interests. These are important factors that complement more technical considerations when gauging the overall supply versus demand approaches.

That said, the demand-side of the in-kind versus cash debate can be summarized by school feeding versus CCT programs, both of which are largely geared toward education objectives. School feeding programs are among the largest education-related, in-kind transfer schemes globally. The volume of spending is about USD 75 billions annually and these programs have been widely used also in humanitarian contexts: for example, during the 2007/08 food and fuel crises at least 38 low and middle income countries scaled-up their school feeding schemes (WFP 2013). These interventions, which can take the form of school meals and take home rations, are currently present in 131 countries and reach 105 million beneficiaries in India, 47 million in Brazil, and 26 in China—and about 375 million people around the world. Conversely, CCTs are implemented in 64 countries, with the largest-scale schemes reach 49 million beneficiaries in Brazil, 26 million in Mexico and 19 million in the Philippines (World Bank 2015).

Just like CCTs, school feeding can generally pursue a mix of objectives in enhancing education as well as nutrition, provide an income transfer, and more recently in promotion of agriculture through "home grown school feeding" (Sumberg and Sabates-Wheeler 2011). The first of these objectives is regularly met, including in terms of attendance and reduction in school-drop out (Bundy et al. 2009). Nutritional impacts, however, are less often documented, in part because the age group reached directly is less at risk of undernutrition than are younger children. Moreover, given trends in obesity, it is not even clear what gains should be monitored. There are similar findings emerging in the extensive empirical literature around CCTs (Fiszbein and Schady 2009; Ravallion 2016; World Bank 2014).

As Alderman and Bundy (2012) put it, school feeding "… is a plausible candidate for a social protection investment on a par with CCTs." Precisely for this reasons, it is remarkable that, considering also the massive scale of the programs, there is virtually no comparative impact evaluation that contrasts school feeding to CCTs in attaining educational goals.

Shelter

According to a recent position paper, the increasing momentum behind cash transfers in general, and unconditional multi sector grants in particular, does not take into consideration some of the specifics, complexities and technical challenges of shelter programming (GSC 2015). One key issue concerns the stage in crisis. While providing cash can allow people to find short term rented accommodation or purchase materials for temporary or emergency shelters, cash approaches for the medium-term have raised concerns. This centers on risks, liabilities and quality standards related to construction of more permanent shelter as part of the early recovery and reconstruction phases (Juillard and Opu 2014).

Relatedly, the high-value payments that result from "cashing-out" shelter support may amplify protection risks. As in other sectors, there is a strong need for monitoring, communication and engagement with communities to ensure a clear understanding program objectives beyond getting families "under a roof," including forging a shared vision between communities and humanitarian actors. Some initial pilots, however, show that some of those challenges can be overcome with incentives-based design (see box 4.4).

Box 4.4 Piloting Cash for Shelter Needs

In urban contexts in Jordan, a cash grant was designed to cover shelter needs for 4,000 Syrian refugee households. It is using a combination of the following: (i) a phased conditional cash grants for landlords who are asked to complete unfinished buildings or rooms and to host Syrian refugees for a year and a half (for free); and (ii) unconditional payments to refugee households to cover move-in fees and basic furniture.

In the Philippines, an nongovernmental organization (NGO) implemented a cash grant for shelter. After implementation, monitoring data highlighted that much of the grant intended for shelter was being spent to cover household's food needs. This led to restructuring of the

---

box continues next page

Box 4.4 Piloting Cash for Shelter Needs *(continued)*

intervention as follows: a single transfer of PhP 5,000 for food and basic needs to be deter-
mined by the household; a conditional cash grant for shelter, delivered in three tranches, with
later tranches provided once progress in the construction of the shelter was confirmed; and a
single livelihoods grant of PhP 6,700, provided after attendance at skills training and development of a business proposal. Subsequent monitoring found that 96 percent of families then
spent their shelter money on shelter and that the household didn't have other unmet needs.

During the peak of the Haitian displacement crisis, more than 1.5 million people were living in over 1,500 camps; in early 2013, these were reduced to 320,000 people living in 385
camps. The Rental Support Cash Grant aimed to help closing the cycle of displacement and
putting families back to living conditions comparable to those pre-earthquake. Despite the
huge scale of the displacement, the program enabled over 500,000 Haitians to leave un-
planned displacement camps. In particular, it provided financial payments to displaced fami-
lies/individuals for a fixed-term lease in accommodation rented from a private-sector land-
lord. Housing conditions were subject to rigorous assessment, including only allowing those
classified as viable or "green" to be part of the program. Cash grants included $500 per family,
$25 for transport costs, and an unconditional $125 if the family was still in the rental property
6–8 weeks after the program. A decision was made early on to assess vulnerability and needs
using camps as the unit of analysis. In other words, if a camp was judged to be a priority for
assistance, all the families inside that camp would benefit from the program. After a process of
registration and communication, implementing agency staff guided the beneficiary to a low
cost rental property of choice. The agency member may choose to pay beneficiaries through
banks, or through mobile phone money applications. The next step is the relocation, and the
need to dismantle tents and closing the camp to avoid among other, security and health risks.
Haitian protection teams were however mainstreamed into all steps of the process.

An overall national housing market encompasses a constellation of individual
markets, and it is essential to gain an understanding of their dynamics. This
includes the capacity of the construction industry, the volume of useable housing
stock for purchase or rent, availability of land, key construction materials, skilled
and unskilled labor, credit, loans, mortgages and other housing finance mechanisms. In crisis contexts, tracking key shelter markets such as the rental sector has
proven significantly complex, and the shelter sector and, at the moment, the
broader humanitarian community does not seem to possess the means or capacity to produce such assessments in any systematic manner. However, the same set
of considerations can apply to in-kind provisions, that is, in-kind transfers for
shelter should also be informed by market assessments.

Cross-Sectoral or "Multi-Purpose" Transfers

The concept of multi-purpose cash transfers (MPCT) is a recent innovation envi-
sioning the provision of cash to individuals for an amount large enough to cover

several needs that transcend sectoral boundaries (for example, food security, health, education, shelter). Arguably, several contextual factors driving cost efficiency and effectiveness around food security transfers, for example, can be extended to MPCTs. Also, some of the evidence presented around livelihoods could be relevant for this transfer model. For instance, the grant programs described in box 4.2 provide a range of interventions that add-up to a grant, but these are generally geared to pursue a core objective, not a multitude of them.

As a result, multi-sectoral programs present specific features, including in terms of design, monitoring, reporting, coordination, and evaluation parameters. While a discussion of the conceptual and operational feasibility of such programs goes beyond the scope of this paper, we note that there is a limited, if any, evidence on comparative impacts relative to in-kind grants.

Following Maunder et al. (2015), "… no quantitative evidence was found from research, evaluations or comparative studies—reflecting the relatively new status of both MPCTs and cost efficiency analysis—and there is a need to generate more quantitative evidence." In addition, the authors further argued that:

> not all needs can be effectively addressed through a single consolidated transfer—certain, specific needs may be more appropriately addressed through single sector transfers as a complement to MPCTs—such as shelter and nutrition. Consequently a need for multiple agencies and programs may remain and cost efficiency gains will be limited.

Notes

1. CaLP Cash Atlas online database (accessed February 2016). The figure also includes livelihood interventions.
2. A new experimental study by Ahmed et al. (2016) will soon be released, including comparing cash, food and several combined modalities (and with and without nutritional information campaigns) in Bangladesh.
3. When provided individually, transfers didn't exceed targets.
4. Food consumption can be measured in terms of consumption or expenditures. Food expenditures are the amount of money spent on food in any given time period, while food consumption is the value of food actually consumed during the given time period. Food consumption/expenditures can be constructed in reference to daily, monthly or yearly values.
5. Leroy et al. (2010) recommended that in order to avoid overconsumption of energy,

   > programs should not be implemented without an effective behavior change communication component … [and] the use of low-fat milk (…) or the use of micronutrient supplements not containing energy, such as micronutrient sprinkles, should be considered as alternatives in this program. (616)

6. The Dietary Diversity Index (DDI) is the number of different foods or food groups consumed over a given reference period. The Food Consumption Scores (FCS) index is calculated using the frequency of consumption of eight food groups consumed by

a household during the seven days before the survey. The Household Dietary Diversity Score (HDDS) is a proxy indicator of household food access. The score is calculated by summing the number of food groups consumed in the previous seven days from 12 groups. It differs from the DDI in that frequency is measured across standardized food groups instead of individual food items. Among other factors, it differs from the FCS in that the reference period is one day and not seven, and it does not take into account the frequency of food consumption (and it is not weighted).

7. In Democratic Republic of Congo (DRC), the size of the voucher transfer in the first distribution was over twice that of Ecuador (USD 90 versus USD 40), while the subsequent two installments were half the Ecuador's value (USD 20 versus USD 40). The Ecuador project envisaged 6 monthly distributions, while the ones in the DRC only three over 7 months (see table 4.2). Also, in the latter vouchers could being freely spent on foods available, while in Ecuador there were caps on spending by food groups (for example, out of USD 40, a maximum of USD 10 could be spent on cereals).

8. In the first of three distribution cycles, vouchers could be used for food and non-food items, while in the latter two for food only. Under the project, vouchers could being freely spent on all foods available in the fairs, while in Ecuador there were caps on spending by food groups (for example, out of USD 40, a maximum of USD 10 could be spent on cereals).

9. For example, a project costing a total of EUR 30 million delivers USD 20 million in transfers to beneficiaries (and spends USD 10 million on administrative costs), the Total Cost-Transfer Ratio (TCTR) is 30/20 or 1.5.

10. Cabot Venton, Bailey, and Pongracz (2015) document that, in Ethiopia, the cost of local food is typically lower than international food aid in the harvest season, but international food prices can be cheaper than local prices in the lean season. In the Philippines, local procurement was 27 percent less costly than overseas food aid once transport was considered; in Lebanon, instead, the cost of hygiene items and non-food items is much cheaper when procured internationally in bulk.

11. The question is part of larger investigation around how people behave in the presence of poverty traps and under-investment, if there are "self-control" problems and time-inconsistent preferences (for example, if an individual prefers that tomorrow he or she reinvests profits in the business, but when tomorrow comes prefers to spend the money), or the occurrence of coordination failures, such as when there is a discrepancy between perceived and expected returns to training (De Mel, McKenzie, and Woodruff 2012).

12. Clemens and Pritchett (2016) put those impacts in perspective and compared them to the possible gains stemming from migration: "a two-year, six-component in situ intervention [which increased per capita consumption by US$54 per year] produced the equivalent annual consumption gain of the wage differentials of working in a rich versus poor country for one day."

13. Objectives of nutrition actions in emergencies typically include reducing levels of wasting (global acute malnutrition and severe acute malnutrition with or without oedema) to below conventionally-defined emergency rates or thresholds; reducing and/or preventing micronutrient deficiencies, because these markedly increase mortality; (reducing the specific vulnerability of infants and young children in crises through the promotion of appropriate child care, with special emphasis on infant and young child feeding practices; and preventing a life-threatening deterioration of

nutritional status by ensuring access by emergency-affected populations to adequate, safe and nutritious foods that meet minimum nutrient needs; these should be assessed in relation to the prevailing disease burden, pre-existing nutrient deficiencies, temperature considerations, and others.

14. Conditional cash transfers (CCTs) may vary considerably in terms of level of planning, monitoring, and enforcement of compliance. For example, the World Bank (2015) distinguishes four categories of conditionalities with respect to education-related conditions: (i) explicit conditions on paper and/or encouragement of children's schooling, but no monitoring or enforcement (an example is Ecuador's Bono de Desarollo Humano); (i) explicit conditions, monitored with minimal enforcement (examples are Brazil's Bolsa Familia and Mexico's Prospera); (iii) explicit conditions with monitoring and enforcement of enrollment condition (an example is Cambodia's Scholarship Program); and (iv) explicit conditions with monitoring and enforcement of attendance condition (examples are Malawi's Schooling, Income and HIV Risk CCT arm and China's Pilot CCT program).

CHAPTER 5

Factors to Consider in Transfer Selection

Against the background of the previous chapters, we distill six main factors to consider for appropriate decision-making in selecting between transfer modalities. These have been extensively discussed in the literature and include program objectives, the level of market functionality, predicted cost-effectiveness, implementation capacity, protection and gender, and political economy (DFID 2013; ECHO 2013; Gentilini 2016; Harvey and Bailey 2011; Lentz et al. 2013; Levine and Bailey 2015; UNHCR 2012; WFP 2015a, b).

Objectives and Initial Conditions

Setting clear objectives is key for gauging performance as they are the lens through which effectiveness and efficiency are examined. In a number of cases, programs can pursue multiple objectives and it would be important to lay them out as specifically as possible as well as prioritize them. For example, just pursuing "food security" objectives may not be very informative, and practitioners may consider focusing on specific dimensions such as calories availability or dietary diversity. In the case of cash, the setting of specific metrics becomes key to ensure appropriate performance measurement: while cash is fungible, fungibilty is not an impact per se but a feature of the modality.

The setting of objectives should also be closely aligned with beneficiaries' profiles. Accounting for "Initial conditions" plays a key role in clarifying the objectives of the cash or in-kind program and interpret results. This is closely related to considerations around targeting and setting realistic expectations for what a modality can achieve for people with different characteristics. Our discussion around livelihoods showed that it is harder to achieve entrepreneurial results when cash or in-kind grants are provided to the poorest. Similarly, the starting point of beneficiaries in terms of, say, calories availability, may likely affect the size of impacts: where the initial level of calories is very low, we may probably observe an impact of larger size compared to the effects on households whose initial level of calories is higher (Asfaw 2006; Leroy et al. 2010). Hidrobo et al. (2014a) present evidence on this relationship: based on a meta-analysis of evaluations of transfer programs, the authors show that impacts tend to decrease by about 2 percent every increase in 100 kilocalories at baseline.

Finally, the setting of objectives should be the result of a nuanced understanding of the determinants of a given problem. It can be argued that the humanitarian imperative motivating the provision of cash or in-kind assistance in the 2–3 weeks following a disaster poses particular pressure for swift action. This implies that the depth and breadth of response analysis would range from basic analysis in the immediate aftermath of disasters, to more sophisticated and comprehensive processes as emergencies get prolonged and protracted. Those approaches should be nested within a theory of change on why and how transfers will affect a given dimension, particularly around nutrition, health, education and shelter issues. In other words, the setting of objectives should be closely intertwined with a process of understanding the causes of the problem at hand and how to address it.

Understanding Markets

Turning "needs" into "effective demand" is a key rationale for cash transfers. Yet this might be challenging in presence of weakly-integrated or poorly-competitive markets. In those contexts, price transmissions across areas might be fragmented and hampered by policy or physical bottlenecks (for example, trade policy, damage of roads and infrastructure, limited information, or hoarding practices), and localized cash injections may result in price spikes leaving consumers or net buyers worse-off. In other words, there are circumstances where local markets may perform poorly, food prices may be excessively high or volatile, and private traders may not have incentives to supply commodities. In those contexts, a cash transfer may neither lead to more choice nor purchasing power, and in-kind food may be a more appropriate response (that is, it ensures both availability of and access to food). From this perspective, a basic level of market functioning is a *prerequisite* for the effective provision of cash transfers and to enable local economic multipliers.

The discussion on market analysis has important practical implications for program design, implementation and efficiency. In some cases, price forecasts may be particularly uncertain in the program design stage. These could turn a program that was efficient in the planning phase into a cost-inefficient one during implementation. Indeed, keeping purchasing power constant in the wake of sharp price increases may escalate costs due to extensive use of contingency funds, such as shown in Zambia (Harvey and Savage 2006). Similar issues are also faced in contexts of more predictable price dynamics: in Malawi, for example, analysis on price trends over 20 years shows mean inter-seasonal price fluctuations in the order of 60 percent (Ellis and Manda 2012).

While understanding food markets, supply chains and demand dynamics is no easy task, standards and tools are being developed to measure a "working market" and link it to response analysis (Barrett et al. 2009; Michelson et al. 2012). As cash is becoming more "intersectoral" and used to pursue multiple objectives across traditional sectors, this raises the question of how to ensure a comprehensive assessment of markets beyond food, and including for example shelter markets.

Expected Cost-Effectiveness

The expected cost-effectiveness of alternative transfers is challenging to predict. But as evidence is increasing (that is, for food security), decision-makers can begin observe a mild tendency on what to expect from a given transfer. This would help anticipate the likelihood of objectives being achieved. New tools are now being developed to help inform such ex-ante decision-making process of calibrating anticipated effectiveness (Ryckembusch et al. 2013).

Clearly, the effectiveness equation has many variable, and many of them would depend on a host of design issues. These may include the characteristics of targeted beneficiaries (see discussion on objectives), the size of transfers, the duration of programs, the timing and frequency of payments, household expenditure patterns, the commodities that constitute the composition of food baskets, and how manages resources at household level. These decisions may actually shape effectiveness more than the modality of transfers (Levine and Bailey 2015). Potential negative impacts should also be anticipated and managed—for example, on food prices or intracommunity relations (MacAuslan and Riemenschneider 2011)—as well as possible externalities such as economic multipliers (FAO 2015).

As we have seen, the issue of cost can be less straightforward than often assumed. The nuances around scale of interventions, the presence of common platforms, type of humanitarian crisis, procurement costs, and a host of hidden costs all call for more comprehensive costs assessments than those based on sole delivery costs. Also in this case, costs should be interpreted against objectives. Especially when it comes to humanitarian situations, there might be circumstances where higher costs could be justified on life-saving grounds, but these should take into account alternatives more systematically.

Both effectiveness and efficiency considerations should take into account risks. Different transfers might entail different risks, including around security, corruption or diversion, delays in providing transfers and market failures, or protection (see point discussed below). If a transfer modality was rejected because of identified risks, decision-makers should consider whether these or comparable risks existed for other choices, if the risks could be managed, and whether an unjustified degree of risk aversion was shown and hindered program cost-effectiveness.

Implementation Capacity

A number of humanitarian actors may have more experience managing in-kind transfers than other modalities. There is, though, a responsibility to provide appropriate assistance, and so choices should not be justified based only on pre-existing skills and experience. However, it might be unreasonable to expect capacity to deliver "new" transfer types to be built up immediately or during a massive, urgent emergency response.

Also in this case, the global trends in humanitarian situations being increasingly protracted suggests that crises should be dealt with a longer operational timeframe, not just with a 6–12 months lens. Two considerations emerge: on one hand, there is a clear opportunity to link with existing national safety nets when possible. This would imply a nuanced analysis of local government implementation capacities across the delivery spectrum. On the other hand, technology is helping to leap-frog a number of traditional bottlenecks that hamper operational processes.

Yet innovations in identification through biometrics, the use of smart cards and phones for payments, and e-tools for monitoring affect all modalities, whether food, cash or vouchers. For example, a growing share pf vouchers are now digital and delivered through phones (for example, Syrian Arab Republic and Zambia) and swipe cards (for example, Palestine), hence sharply reducing the administrative burden that paper-based models entailed (Omamo, Gentilini, and Sandstrom 2010). Food transfers increasingly use satellite technology to map and track movements throughout supply chains[1]; at the same time, the delivery of cash transfers is also increasingly moving away from hard cash, on-site distributions to various versions of digital payments. In other words, the backbone of technology across delivery systems is increasingly putting transfers to somewhat an equal footing, and particularly so when it comes to compare cash transfers and voucher. This doesn't mean that differences cease to exist, but it puts even more pressure on quality of design as a key aspect in spurring comparative effectiveness and efficiency (see previous discussion).

Protection and Gender

The transfer and delivery mechanism should be acceptable and accessible to those who face constraints, including issues related to gender, age and other factors that might affect access to assistance. The effect of transfers on the safety, dignity and integrity of recipients should have been constantly considered. No intervention can guarantee an absence of risk, but decision-makers should be able to show that they have considered risks related to protection (that is, social tensions, intra-household dynamics) and balance those considerations against the short and medium-term effects on empowerment and social norms.

Political Economy

Although technical considerations should be the first-order considerations, political economy factors play an important role. This may not only include societal values and interests among both donor and receiving governments, but also specific preferences by beneficiaries. We briefly discussed this point in chapter 2, including how those preferences are not fixed over space, time and individuals. This is also related to the more prosaic question of resource availability: while in an ideal world technical decision-making process would determine transfer modalities, in practice the availability of certain modalities may influence decision making by tiling it toward what's feasible instead of what's desirable. This is particularly compelling for large scale, humanitarian operations that often find themselves relatively underfunded compared to needs.

Note

1. The Logistics Execution Support System (LESS) is a new tool launched by WFP that is able to locate food commodities in real-time, including when they are shipped, unloaded in ports, stocked in warehouses, or distributed to beneficiaries. LESS covers the entire food supply chain by integrating programmatic, financial, procurement and logistics functions. With real-time tracking capabilities, LESS provides precise information on food stock quantities and locations, which is key for planning and preparedness for scale-up in emergencies. The information allows better management in many areas. For example, it keeps track of best-before and use-by dates on food stock. This helps managers to intervene earlier to avoid waste by diverting underutilized stock in a particular project. LESS can also assist in the event of a product recall since it can track exactly in which warehouse, or even on which truck, a specific batch from a vendor is located. The system was successfully adopted in Afghanistan and Pakistan in October 2014 and by the end of 2016 it will be mainstreamed worldwide (WFP 2015b).

CHAPTER 6

Evidence Gaps and Research Priorities

In order to identify evidence gaps and applied research priorities, we consider a basic metric of "level of evidence" as measured by the number of comparative randomized controlled trials, quasi-experimental evaluations, and other robust quantitative methods utilized for the generation of evidence. This, of course, should be interpreted with caution, including due to the possible limitations stemming from external validity (or generalization of results), and because of the inherent limits of conducting scientific research in humanitarian contexts. At the same time, where such evidence level is relatively rich, we observe the emergence of somewhat consistent patterns in findings. We also notice recent efforts to bolster evidence-generation in the humanitarian space or in similar challenging circumstances. This seems promising especially for protracted crises, although it holds obvious limitations for sudden, covariate disasters and areas affected by conflict.

Against this background, we define as "substantial" the evidence base informed by more than 10 solid comparative evaluations that contrast cash, in-kind and/or vouchers. In cases where such number is between 5 and 10, the evidence can be considered "emerging," while if only a handful (or lower than 5) it may be deemed "limited." Where no evaluations were available, evidence is clearly "absent" (table 6.1).

What is the level of evidence across the examined objectives? It can be reasonably argued that food security objectives have an overall substantial evidence base, although stronger for impacts than for costs. For livelihoods objectives, the

Table 6.1 Relative Level of Comparative Evidence

No. of Evaluations	Level of Evidence
None	Absent
From 1 to 5	Limited
From 6 to 9	Emerging
10 and above	Substantial

Source: Author's compilation.

Table 6.2 Level of Comparative Evidence by Objective

Objective	Overall Evidence Base	Impacts or Effectiveness	Costs or Efficiency
Food security	Substantial	Substantial	Emerging
Livelihoods	Emerging	Emerging	Limited
Nutrition	Limited	Limited	Limited
Health	Absent	Absent	Absent
Education	Absent	Absent	Absent
Shelter	Absent	Absent	Absent
Multisector	Absent	Absent	Absent

Source: Author's compilation.

general state of the evidence is emerging, although also in this case with relatively larger gaps in comparative cost assessments (table 6.2). The issue of comprehensive and comparative cost analyses in food security objectives should be carefully considered given the sheer size of interventions in that domain.

For nutrition, we have documented some comparative studies, including in relation to micronutrients and child severe and acute malnutrition. Based on the available studies, the evidence based is defined as limited. For the "services-oriented" objectives of health and education, there is a clear evidence gap in both impacts and costs, with the resulting evidence base being absent or unavailable. Comparative evidence is equally lacking for shelter and multisectoral approaches such as multi-purpose cash transfers.

CHAPTER 7

Conclusions

This paper reviews the existing evidence on the performance of alternative transfer modalities across humanitarian objectives or sectors. The analysis focused on the *comparative* performance of transfers, that is, to studies that employed robust statistical methods to assess transfers against each other. This allows not only to understand how transfers work in general, but which works best relative to the other. We did so for a variety of objectives which generally match the humanitarian clusters. Based on existing evidence, we identified possible criteria for transfer selection and key priority areas for future research. Taken together, our analysis suggests five main conclusions.

First, there is large variance in the availability of comparative evidence across sectors. This ranges from areas where evidence is substantial (that is, food security) to realms where it is limited (that is, nutrition) or where not a single comparative evaluation was available (that is, health, education, and shelter). This unbalance should be carefully considered when devising interventions and reforms that affect both single and multiple humanitarian sectors.

Second, where evidence is substantial, like for the food security cluster, data shows mixed results for cash and in-kind transfers, that is, their effectiveness is similar on average. Specific differences among cash and in-kind transfers are not very significant and depend on sub-objectives (for example, calories availability, dietary diversity) and indicators used to measure them. Also, transfers' performance and their difference seem a function of the organic and fluid interactions among a number of factors (for example, profile and "initial conditions" of beneficiaries, capacity of local markets), instead of inherent merits of one modality over the other.

Third, while the effectiveness of cash and food is similar, the efficiency is generally in favor of cash. Cash transfers seem more efficient to *deliver* than in-kind modalities, suggesting it might be more cost-effective on average. However, results should be interpreted with caution, including because of the wealth of nuance that is often not captured in standard costs analysis. Delivery is only one dimension of cost assessments, and overall costs would hinge on the scale of interventions, crisis context, procurement practices, and hidden costs. Approaches for cost calculations are often not standardized and display high variance in the depth and breadth of analysis. More consistent and robust approaches are required so that efficiency analyses match the high-standards of effectiveness as offered by the examined impact evaluations. Whether in terms of effectiveness or efficiency, the use of combined transfers seems a promising and yet under-evaluated program model.

Fourth, the appropriateness of transfers cannot be predetermined—there are no "first-best" options from the outset, but rather first-best options are context-specific and emerge from careful response analysis. We distilled main factors to consider for appropriate decision-making in selecting between transfer modalities. These have been extensively discussed the empirical and operational literature and include program objectives, the level of market functionality, predicted cost-effectiveness, implementation capacity, the management of key risks such as on protection and gender, political economy, beneficiary preferences, and resource availability. The depth and breadth of response analysis would range from basic analysis in the immediate aftermath of disasters, to more sophisticated and comprehensive processes as emergencies get prolonged and protracted.

Finally, it seems possible to reconcile humanitarian imperatives with more and better research to fill key information gaps. Given the nature of humanitarian situations, it is understandable that in many circumstances "action cannot wait for evidence." Notwithstanding humanitarian imperatives, as crises become more chronic and protracted there is an important case to be made to synchronize careful response analysis, operations, and a solid applied research agenda to compare performance of alternative transfer modalities. Many of the cases in challenging environments presented in the note, for example, the Democratic Republic of Congo (DRC), Niger, and the Republic of Yemen, show that such analysis is possible and necessary to serve people in need in the best way possible.

Features of Comparative Impact Evaluations of Food Security Modalities

Program	Country	Program Type*	Modality	Cash Size (USD)	Size as % of pre-program HH exp.	Transfer Frequency	HH Size	Exposure	Delivery Mechanism	Sample Size (HHs at end line)	Evaluation Method	Reference
PAL	Mexico	CT, UT	Cash, Food[a]	13	11.5	Monthly (cash), bi-monthly (food)	4.2	1 year	Biometric debit cards	(a) 5,028 (b) 5,851 (c) 5,823	DD DD DD	(a) Cunha (2014) (b) Skoufias, Unar, and Gonzalez-Cossio(2012) (c) Leroy et al. (2010)
Zinder project	Niger	PW, UT	Cash, Food[b]	50	11.5	Bi-weekly	7	6 months	Mobile ATMs, smart cards	2,209	SD	Hoddinott, Sandstrom, and Upton (2014)
Acute malnutrition intervention	Niger	UT	Cash, Food, Cash + Food[k]	59	n.a.	Monthly	n.a.	5 months	n.a.	5,395	Prospective cohort	Langendorf et a. (2014)
PSNP	Ethiopia	PW, UT	Cash, Food[c]	16.2	n.a.	Monthly	5	6 months per year	N/A	960	SD	Sabates-Wheeler and Devereux (2010)
Early childhood development program	Uganda	CT	Cash, Food[d]	10.2	12.7	6–8 week cycle	6.2	12 months	Mobile money cards	2,461	ANCOVA	Gilligan and Roy (2013)
Colombian refugees project	Ecuador	CT	Cash, Food[e], Vouchers	40	10	Monthly	3.8	6 months	ATM card	2,122	ANCOVA	Hidrobo et al. (2014b)
IDPs project	Democratic Republic of Congo	UT	Cash, Vouchers[f]	18.5	18.96	Bi-monthly	5.5	7 months	Bank accounts	252	Fixed effects	Aker (2015)
Unconditional safety net	Yemen	UT	Cash, Food[g]	49	n.a.	Bi-monthly	7.9	6 months	ID card via Postal Savings Corporation	1,581	SD, ANCOVA, DD, DDD	Schwab (2013)

table continues next page

Program	Country	Program Type*	Modality	Cash Size (USD)	Size as % of Ore-program HH exp.	Transfer Frequency	HH Size	Exposure	Delivery Mechanism	Sample Size (HHs at end line)	Evaluation Method	Reference
Scholarship pilot program	Cambodia	CT	Cash, Food[g]	5	2.5	Monthly	6	10 months	On-site manual distribution	4,091	DD	Barker, Filmer, and Rigolini (2014)
Cash transfer pilot program	Sri Lanka	UT	Cash, Food[i]	9.8	26.3	Bi-weekly (cash), bi-monthly (food)	3.8	3 months	Samurdhi Bank	1,357 s	DD	Sharma (2006)
IGVGD, RMP	Bangladesh	UT, PW	Cash, Food[j]	19.7	30 (cash) 15.5 (food)	Bi-monthly (cash), monthly (food)	4.6	2–4 years	Public banks	1,200	PSM	Ahmed et al. (2010)
Cash and Food for Livelihoods Pilot	Malawi	n.a.	Cash, Food, Cash + Food*	n.a.	n.a.	Monthly		8 months	MSB ATMs	3,542–4,006	RCT	Audsley et al. (2010)

Source: Gentilini (2016)

Note: CT= conditional transfer; UT = unconditional transfer; PW = public works; IDPs = Internally Displaced Persons; n.a. = not applicable; PSM = propensity score matching; RCT = randomized controlled trial; DD = double-difference; IGVGD = Income-Generating Vulnerable Group Development; RMP = Rural Maintenance Program; PAL = Program de Apoyo Alimentario; PSNP = Productive Safety Net Programme.

a. Seven basic items—enriched corn flour, rice, beans, dried pasta soup, biscuits, fortified milk powder, and vegetable oil—and two to four supplementary items (including canned sardines, canned tuna fish, dried lentils, chocolate, breakfast cereal, or corn starch.

b. 3.5 kilograms of grain (primarily maize in the first transfer period and sorghum in the second), 0.72 kilograms of pulses (cowpeas, red beans, or lentils), 0.14 kilograms of vegetable oil, and 0.035 kilograms of salt.

c. 3 kilograms of cereals, plus pulses and oils.

d. Food basket of approximately 1,200 calories, includes corn soy blend ("CSB" – highly fortified with iron among other nutrients), vitamin-A fortified oil, and sugar.

e. The food basket was valued according to regional market prices at USD 40 and included rice (24 kilograms), vegetable oil (4 liters), lentils (8 kilograms), and canned sardines (8 cans of 0.425 kilograms) (voucher: The list of approved foods consists of cereals, tubers, fruits, vegetables, legumes, meats, fish, milk products, and eggs).

f. three food fairs, where participants could get palm oil, sugar, cassava flour, beans, rice, vegetable oil, dried fish, salt, potatoes and peanuts.

g. For an average household size of seven persons is 50 kilograms of wheat flour and 5.0 liters of vegetable oil.

h. 10 kilograms of rice per month.

i. 1.4 kilograms Rice, 1.4 kilograms Wheat flour, 0.42 kilograms Pulses, 0.14 kilograms Oil, 0.14 kilograms Sugar, 0.14 kilograms Corn soy blend.

j. up to 20 kilograms (kg) of wheat or 16 kilograms of rice per month.

k. food included lipid-based nutrients and fortified, super-cereals (50 kilograms), pulses (7.5 kilograms), oil (2.5 kilograms);

*Cereals (50 kilograms), pulses (5 kilograms).

Absolute Differences in Impacts in Food Security (percentage points)

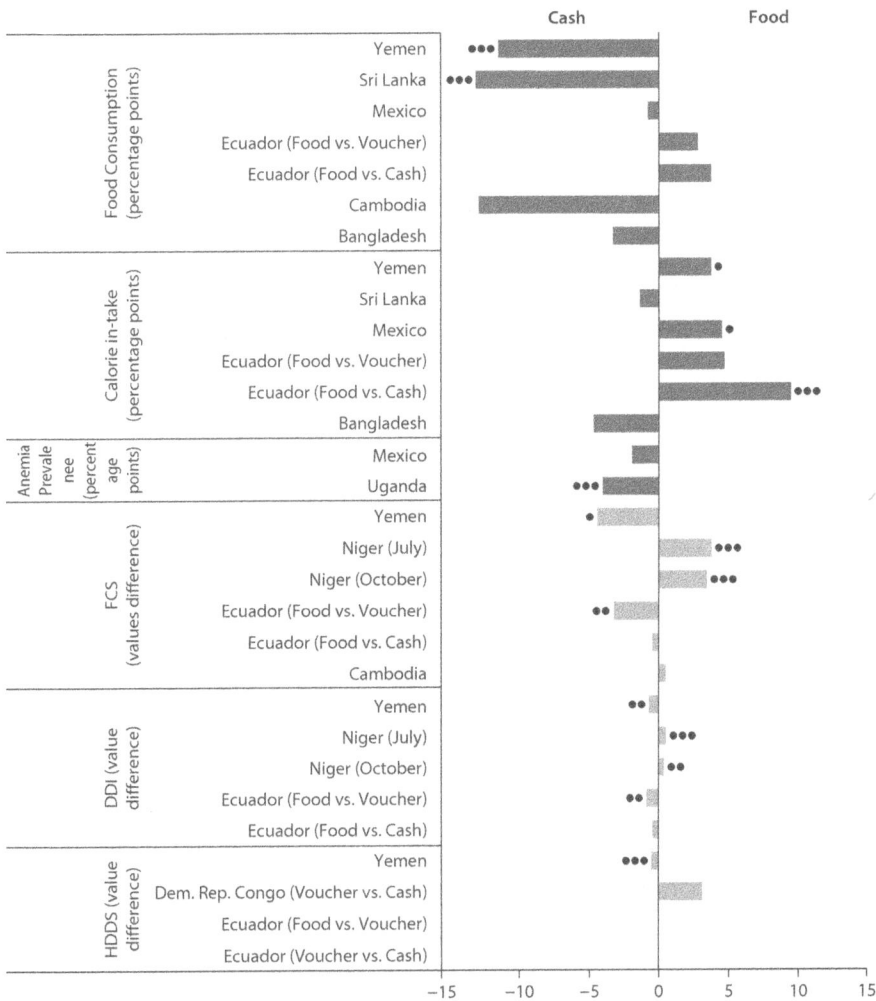

Cash · Food

Food Consumption (percentage points)
- Yemen ●●●
- Sri Lanka ●●●
- Mexico
- Ecuador (Food vs. Voucher)
- Ecuador (Food vs. Cash)
- Cambodia
- Bangladesh

Calorie in-take (percentage points)
- Yemen ·
- Sri Lanka
- Mexico ·
- Ecuador (Food vs. Voucher)
- Ecuador (Food vs. Cash) ●●●
- Bangladesh

Anemia Prevalenee (percentage points)
- Mexico
- Uganda ●●●

FCS (values difference)
- Yemen ·
- Niger (July) ●●●
- Niger (October) ●●●
- Ecuador (Food vs. Voucher) ●●
- Ecuador (Food vs. Cash)
- Cambodia

DDI (value difference)
- Yemen ●●
- Niger (July) ●●●
- Niger (October) ●●
- Ecuador (Food vs. Voucher) ●●
- Ecuador (Food vs. Cash)

HDDS (value difference)
- Yemen ●●●
- Dem. Rep. Congo (Voucher vs. Cash)
- Ecuador (Food vs. Voucher)
- Ecuador (Voucher vs. Cash)

−15 −10 −5 0 5 10 15

Source: Gentilini (2016)

Note: Bars in dark-gray refer to difference in percentage points, light-gray bars refer to changes in specific indicator values. Level of significance in differences is indicated by asterisks (* at 90% level, ** at 9% level, *** at 99 percent level).
DDI = Dietary Diversity Index; HDDS = Household Dietary Diversity Score; FCS = Food Consumption Scores..

References

Ahmed, A., A. Quisumbing, M. Nasreen, J. Hoddinott, and E. Bryan. 2010. "Comparing Food and Cash Transfers to the Ultra Poor in Bangladesh." *Research Monograph* 163. Washington, DC: IFPRI.

Ahmed, A., J. Hoddinott, S. Roy, E. Sraboni, W. Quabili, and A. Margolies. 2016. "Which Kind of Social Safety Net Transfers Work Best for the Ultra Poor in Bangladesh? Operation and Impacts of the Transfer Modality Research Initiative." Dhaka: IFPRI and WFP.

Aker, J. 2015. "Comparing Cash and Vouchers in a Humanitarian Context: Evidence from the Democratic Republic of Congo." *World Bank Policy Research*, Working Paper 7469.

Alderman, H., and D. Bundy. 2012. "School Feeding Programs and Development: Are We Framing the Question Correctly?" *World Bank Research Observer* 27 (2): 204–21.

Almeida, R., J. Behrman, and D. Robalino. 2012. *The Right Skills for the Job? Rethinking Training Policies for Workers*, edited by World Bank. Washington, DC: World Bank.

ALNAP. 2015. *The State of the Humanitarian System – 2015 Edition*. London.

Amacher, R., and T., Sandler. 1977. "The Externality Argument for In-Kind Transfers: A Defense." *Kyklos* 30 (2): 293–96.

Asfaw, A. 2006. "The Role of Food Price Policy in Determining the Prevalence of Obesity: Evidence from Egypt". *Review of Agricultural Economics* 28 (3): 305–12.

Audsley, B., N. Balzer, and R. Halme. 2010. "Comparing the Efficiency of Cash and Food Transfers: A Cost-Benefit Analysis from Rural Malawi". In *Revolution: From Food Aid to Food Assistance. Innovations in Overcoming Hunger*, edited by S. W. Omamo, U. Gentilini, and S. Sandstrom. Rome: WFP.

Bandiera, O., R. Burgess, N. Das, S. Gulesci, I. Rasul, and M. Sulaiman. 2012. *Can Basic Entrepreneurship Transform the Economic Lives of the Poor?* London: International Growth Centre.

Banerjee, A., E. Duflo, N. Goldberg, D. Karlan, R. Osei, W. Parienté, J. Shapiro, B. Thuysbaert, and C. Udry. 2015. "A Multifaceted Program Causes Lasting Progress for the Very Poor: Evidence from Six Countries." *Science* 348 (6236): 772–90.

Barker, M., D. Filmer, and J. Rigolini. 2014. *Evaluating Food versus Cash Assistance in Rural Cambodia*. Washington, DC: World Bank.

Barrett, C., R. Bell, E. Lentz, and D. Maxwell. 2009. "Market Information and Food Insecurity Response Analysis." *Food Security* 1 (1): 151–168.

Basu, K.. 1996. "Relief Programs: When It May Be Better to Give Food Instead of Cash". *World Development* 24 (1): 91–96.

Blackorby, C., and D. Donaldson. 1988. "Cash Versus Kind, Self-selection, and Efficient Transfers." *American Economic Review* 78 (4): 691–700.

Blattman, C., N. Fiala, and S. Martinez. 2014. "Generating Skilled Self-Employment in Developing Countries: Experimental Evidence from Uganda." *Quarterly Journal of Economics* 129 (2): 697–752.

Blattman, C., J. Jamison, and M. Sheridan. 2015. "Reducing Crime and Violence: Experimental Evidence on Adult Noncognitive Investments in Liberia". *Working Paper* 21204. Cambridge: NBER.

Breunig, R., I. Dasgupta, C. Gundersen, and P. Breuning. 2001. "Explaining the Food Stamp Cash-Out Puzzle." *Food Assistance and Nutrition Research Report* 12. USDA: Washington, DC.

Bundy, D., C. Burbano, M. Grosh, A. Gelli, M. Jukes, and L. Drake. 2009. *Rethinking School Feeding: Social Safety Nets, Child Development and the Education Sector*. Washington, DC: World Bank.

Cabot Venton, C., S. Bailey, and S. Pongracz. 2015. "Value for Money of Cash Transfers in Emergencies." London.

Clemens, M., and L. Pritchett. 2016. "The New Economic Case for Migration Restrictions: An Assessment". *Working Paper* 423. Washington DC: Center for Global Development.

Coate, S. 1989. "Cash versus Direct Food Relief." *Journal of Development Economics* 30 (2): 199–224.

Creti, P. 2011. *The Voucher Programme in the Gaza Strip: Mid-Term Review*. Jerusalem and Oxford: WFP and Oxfam.

Cunha, J. 2014. "Testing Paternalism: Cash versus In-kind Transfers." *American Economic Journal: Applied Economics* 6 (2): 195–230.

Currie, J., and F. Gahvari. 2008. "Transfers in Cash and In-Kind: Theory Meets the Data." *Journal of Economic Literature* 46 (2): 333–83.

De Mel, S., D. McKenzie, and C. Woodruff. 2008. "Returns to Capital in Microenterprises: Evidence from a Field Experiment." *Quarterly Journal of Economics* 123 (4): 1329–72.

De Mel, S., D. McKenzie, and C. Woodruff. 2012. "One-Time Transfers of Cash or Capital Have Long-Lasting Effects on Microenterprises in Sri Lanka." *Science* 335 (962): 962–66.

Devarajan, S. 2013. "Let Them Eat Cash." *Future Development*. https://blogs.worldbank.org/futuredevelopment/let-them-eat-cash.

Devereux, S. 2008. "Innovations in the Design and Delivery of Social Transfers: Lessons Learned from Malawi." Brighton and Dublin: IDS and Concern Worldwide.

DFID. 2013. "Humanitarian Guidance Note: Cash Transfer Programming." London.

ECHO. 2013. *The Use of Cash and Vouchers in Humanitarian Crises. DG ECHO Funding Guidelines*. Brussels.

Ellis, F., and E. Manda. 2012. "Seasonal Food Crises and Policy Responses: A Narrative Account of Three Food Security Crises in Malawi." *Food Policy* 40 (7): 1407–17.

Evans, D., S. Hausladen, K. Kosec, and N. Reese. 2014. *Community based Conditional Cash Transfers in Tanzania: Results from a Randomized Trial*. Washington, DC: World Bank Publications.

Fafchamps, M., D. McKenzie, S. Quinn, and C. Woodruff. 2014. "Microenterprise Growth and the Flypaper Effect: Evidence from a Randomized Experiment in Ghana." *Journal of Development Economics* 106: 211–26.

Faminow, M. 1995. "Issues in Valuing Food Aid: The Cash or In-Kind Controversy." *Food Policy* 20 (1): 3–10.

FAO. 2015. *The State of Food and Agriculture 2015 – Social Protection and Agriculture: Breaking the Cycle of Rural Poverty*. Rome.

Fiala, N. 2013. "Stimulating Microenterprise Growth: Results from a Loans, Grants and Training Experiment in Uganda." Working Paper. Berlin.

Fiszbein, A., and N. Schady. 2009. *Conditional Cash Transfers: Reducing Present and Future Poverty*. Washington, DC: World Bank.

Fraker, T., A. Martini, and J. Ohls. 1995. "The Effect of Food Stamp Cashout on Food Expenditures: An Assessment of the Findings from Four Demonstrations." *Journal of Human Resources* 30 (4): 633–49.

Garfinkel, I. 1973. "Is In-Kind Redistribution Efficient?" *Quarterly Journal of Economics* 87 (2): 320–30.

Gelli, A., and Y. Suwa. 2014. "Investing in Innovation: Trade-offs in the Costs and Cost-efficiency of School Feeding Using Community based Kitchens in Bangladesh." *Food and Nutrition Bulletin* 35 (3): 327–37.

Gentilini, U. 2015. "Entering the City: Emerging Evidence and Practices from Safety Nets in Urban Areas," *Social Protection and Labor Discussion Paper* 1504. Washington, DC: World Bank.

Gentilini, U. 2016. "Revisiting the 'Cash Versus Food' Debate: New Evidence for an Old Puzzle?" *World Bank Research Observer* 31 (1): 135–67.

Gilligan, D., and S. Roy. 2013. "Resources, Stimulation, and Cognition: How Transfer Programs and Preschool Shape Cognitive Development in Uganda." Paper presented at the *Agricultural & Applied Economics Association's 2013 AAEA & CAES Joint Annual Meeting* (August 4–6). Washington, DC.

Gorter, A., C. Grainger, J. Okal, and B. Bellows. 2012. "Systematic Review of Structural and Implementation Issues of Voucher Programs: Analysis of 40 Voucher programs, In-Depth Analysis of 20 Programs." Nairobi: Population Council.

GSC (Global Shelter Cluster). 2015. *Global Shelter Cluster Position Paper: Cash and Markets in the Shelter Sector*. Geneva.

Harvey, P., and S. Bailey. 2011. "Cash Transfer Programming in Emergencies." In *Good Practice Review* 11. London: ODI.

Harvey, P., and K. Savage. 2006. *No Small Change. Oxfam GB Malawi and Zambia Emergency Cash Transfer Projects: A Synthesis of Key Learning*. London: ODI.

Hidrobo, M., J. Hoddinott, N. Kumar, and M. Olivier. 2014a. "Social Protection and Food Security." Background paper prepared for FAO's SOFA report. Washington, DC.

Hidrobo, M., J. Hoddinott, A. Peterman, A. Margolies, and V. Moeira. 2014b. "Cash, Food, or Vouchers? Evidence from a Randomized Experiment in Northern Ecuador." *Journal of Development Economics* 107: 144–56.

Hoddinott, J., S. Sandstrom, and J. Upton. 2014. *The Impact of Cash and Food Transfers: Evidence from a Randomized Intervention in Niger. Discussion Paper* 1341. Washington, DC: IFPRI.

Jensen, R. 2010. "The (Perceived) Returns to Education and the Demand for Schooling." *Quarterly Journal of Economics* 125 (2): 515–48.

Juillard, H., and M. I. Opu. 2014. *Scoping Study: Emergency Cash Transfer Programming in the Wash and Shelter Sectors*. Oxford: CaLP.

Khera, R. 2013. "Revival of the Public Distribution System: Evidence and Explanations." *Economic and Political Weekly* XLVI (44 and 45): 36–50.

Langendorf, C., T. Roederer, S. de Pee, D. Brown, S. Doyon, and A. Mamaty. 2014. "Preventing Acute Malnutrition among Young Children in Crises: A Prospective Intervention Study in Niger." *PLOS Medicine* 11 (9): 2–15.

Lentz, E., C. Barrett, M. Gómez, and D. Maxwell. 2013. "On The Choice and Impacts of Innovative International Food Assistance Instruments." *World Development* 49 (C): 1–8.

Leroy, J., P. Gadsden, S. Rodriguez-Ramirez, and T. Gonzales de Cossio. 2010. "Cash and In-kind Transfers in Poor Rural Communities and Mexico Increase Household Fruit, Vegetable and Micronutrient Consumption but also Lead to Excess Energy Consumption." *Journal of Nutrition* 140 (3): 612–17.

Levine, S., and S. Bailey. 2015. *Cash, Vouchers or In-Kind? Guidance on Evaluating How Transfers Are Made in Emergency Programming*. London: ODI.

MacAuslan, I., and N. Riemenschneider. 2011. "Richer but Resented: What Do Cash Transfers Do To Social Relations?" *IDS Bulletin* 42 (6): 60–66.

Mankiw, G. 2011. *Principles of Microeconomics, 4th Edition*. South-Western: Thomson.

Mankiw, G. 2006. "The Economics of Gifts." http://gregmankiw.blogspot.com.

Margolies, A., and J. Hoddinott. 2014. *Costing Alternative Transfer Modalities*. Washington, DC: IFPRI.

Margolies, A., and J. Hoddinott. 2015. "Costing Alternative Transfer Modalities." *Journal of Development Effectiveness* 7 (1): 1–16.

Maunder, N., N. Dillon, G. Smith, and S. Truelove. 2015 "Evaluation of the Use of Different Transfer Modalities in ECHO Humanitarian Aid Actions 2011–2014." Volumes 1 and 2. Brussels.

Meyer, C., N. Bellows, M. Campbell, and M. Potts. 2011. *The Impact of Vouchers on the Use and Quality of Health Goods and Services in Developing Countries: A Systematic Review*. London: EPPI Centre.

Michelson, H., E. Lentz, M. Mulwa, M. Morey, L. Cramer, M. McGlinchy, and C. Barrett. 2012 "Cash, Food, or Vouchers? An Application of the Market Information and Food Insecurity Response Analysis Framework (MIFIRA) in Urban and Rural Kenya." *Food Security* 4 (3): 455–69.

ODI. 2015. *Doing Cash Differently: How Cash Transfers Can Transform Humanitarian Aid*. London.

Omamo, S. W., U. Gentilini, and S. Sandstrom. 2010. *Revolution: From Food Aid to Food Assistance. Innovations in Overcoming Hunger*, edited by WFP. Rome: WFP.

Ozler, B. 2015. "Should We Just Give People Cash?" In *Policy Research Talk* (presentation, September 29). Washington, DC: World Bank.

Pega, F., S. Y. Liu, S. Walter, and S. K. Lhachimi. 2015. "Unconditional Cash Transfers for Assistance in Humanitarian Disasters: Effect on the Use of Health Services and Health Outcomes in Low and Middle-Income Countries." *Cochrane Database of Systematic Reviews* 9.

Ravallion, M. 2016. *The Economics of Poverty: History, Measurement and Policy*. New York: Oxford University Press.

Reinhart, U. 2013. *On the Economics of Benefits In-Kind.* Princeton, NJ: Princeton University.

Ryckembusch, D., R. Frega, M. B. Da Silva, I. Sanogo, U. Gentilini, N. Grede, and L. Brown. 2013. "Enhancing Nutrition: A New Tool for Ex-Ante Comparison of Commodity-Based Vouchers and Food Transfers." *World Development* 49 (C): 58–67.

Sabates-Wheeler, R., and S. Devereux. 2012. "Cash Transfers and High Food Prices: Explaining Outcomes on Ethiopia's Productive Safety Net Programme." *Food Policy* 35 (4): 274–85.

Sandefur, J., N. Birdsall, and M. Moyo. 2015. "The Political Paradox of Cash Transfers." In *Views from the Center.* Washington, DC: GCD.

Schwab, B. 2013. "In the Form of Bread? A Randomized Comparison of Cash and Food Transfers in Yemen." Paper presented at the *Agricultural & Applied Economics Association's 2013 AAEA & CAES Joint Annual Meeting* (August 4–6, Washington, DC).

Senauer, B., and N. Young. 1986. "The Impact of Food Stamps on Food Expenditures: Rejection of the Traditional Model." *American Journal of Agricultural Economics* 68 (1): 37–43.

Sharma, M. 2006. *An Assessment of the Effects of the Cash Transfer Pilot Project on Household Consumption Patterns in Tsunami-Affected Areas of Sri Lanka.* Washington, DC: IFPRI.

Skoufias, E., M. Unar, and T. Gonzalez-Cossio. 2008. "The Impacts of Cash and In-Kind Transfers on Consumption and Labor Supply: Experimental Evidence from Rural Mexico." *Policy Research Working Paper* 4778. Washington, DC: World Bank.

Southworth, H. 1945. "The Economics of Public Measures to Subsidize Food Consumption." *Journal of Farm Economics* 27 (1):38–66.

Sumberg, J., and R. Sabates-Wheeler. 2011. "Linking Agricultural Development to School Feeding in Sub-Saharan Africa: Theoretical Perspectives." *Food Policy* 36 (3): 341–49.

Tobin, J. 1970. "On Limiting the Domain of Inequality." *Journal of Law and Economics* 13 (2): 263–77.

UNHCR. 2012. *An Introduction to Cash-based Interventions in UNHCR Operations.* Geneva.

UNHCR. 2015. *Cash-based Interventions for Health Programmes in Refugee Settings: A Review.* Geneva.

Webb, P., E. Boyd, S. de Pee, L. Lenters, M. Bloem, and W. Schultink. 2014. "Nutrition in Emergencies: Do We Know What Works?" *Food Policy* 49 (1): 33–40.

WFP. 2013. *The State of School Feeding Worldwide.* Rome.

WFP. 2015a. *Cash and Vouchers Manual: Second Edition.* Rome.

WFP. 2015b. *WFP Logistics in 2014: Excellence in Service Provision.* Rome.

World Bank. 2011. *Social Protection for a Changing India.* New Delhi.

World Bank. 2014. *The State of Social Safety Nets 2014.* Washington, DC.

World Bank. 2015. *The State of Social Safety Nets 2015.* Washington, DC.

World Bank. 2016a. "Strategic Note: Cash Transfers in Humanitarian Contexts." Paper produced for the IASC. Washington, DC.

World Bank. 2016b. *The Digital Dividend: World Development Report 2016.* Washington, DC.

ECO-AUDIT

Environmental Benefits Statement

The World Bank Group is committed to reducing its environmental footprint. In support of this commitment, the Publishing and Knowledge Division leverages electronic publishing options and print-on-demand technology, which is located in regional hubs worldwide. Together, these initiatives enable print runs to be lowered and shipping distances decreased, resulting in reduced paper consumption, chemical use, greenhouse gas emissions, and waste.

The Publishing and Knowledge Division follows the recommended standards for paper use set by the Green Press Initiative. The majority of our books are printed on Forest Stewardship Council (FSC)–certified paper, with nearly all containing 50–100 percent recycled content. The recycled fiber in our book paper is either unbleached or bleached using totally chlorine free (TCF), processed chlorine free (PCF), or enhanced elemental chlorine free (EECF) processes.

More information about the Bank's environmental philosophy can be found at http://crinfo.worldbank.org/wbcrinfo/node/4.